Deborah Mungayi~~nka~~ ~~~~

Truth

—— that ——

Fights

A Survivors' Memoir of the 1994 Genocide against
Tutsi in Kabgayi, Rwanda

Contents

Introduction

I'm sharing my journey with all nations and generations; that Truth fights, and lives not in defeat, but also in victory. This is the Truth that fights daily and continues to struggle against the offshoot of the 1994 genocide against the Tutsi in Rwanda. The Truth that fought yesterday, and fights today, will fight tomorrow and forever; for humanity is God's creation and exists only for His glory. The plan of the enemy was to chase, destroy, steal from me, and eventually kill me, but the Truth shielded me and will shield you, the reader.

The Truth I refer to was what set me free, even when all hope seemed lost. I was rescued in a place named Kabgayi, when it seemed the grave was waiting for me; but the Truth fought and continued the battle until peace was restored. The Word that was used as a weapon, can also fight for you, and give you the peace you require.

The power of life and death is in our tongues and can be a saver in times of trouble. God has a destiny for each one of us, as captured in Jeremiah 29:11: "For I know the thoughts that I think toward you, says the Lord, thoughts of peace and not of evil, to give you an expected end".

This autobiography, to the glory of God, serves as a living testimony to encourage you, my reader, that God is usually beyond our battles. The Truth has brought me out from many deadly circumstances and has helped me to become a peaceful person, filled with happiness.

Acknowledgement

My thanksgiving goes to Almighty God for giving me family and true friends that have encouraged me, and have been very supportive in my dream to achieve this publication.

I equally acknowledge the Rwandan Patriotic Front Army, also known as 'Inkotanyi', who came with strong zeal, courage, and love to rescue me as I was raised from the 'grave' of the 1994 at Saint Joseph College in Kabgayi during the Rwandan Genocide against the Tutsi,.

I acknowledge two churches, New Life International Church Manchester, Arise and Shine Christian Ministries; both situated in the United Kingdom, for their spiritual support that has continued to sustain me. Through them, God has brought the required healing and restoration processes into my life.

The 1994 genocide against the Tutsi in Rwanda, scattered and disorganised my family, and destroyed so much so that it forced us out of our country. But through faith; it has helped us to never throw in the towel.

This project is a product of my daughter, Lesley's curiosity, to get a detailed account of my story, because she once heard me narrating my past experiences to someone and she asked me, "Mum, why did you not tell me all these stories?" I have now chosen to surrender to her request.

My deep appreciation goes to my other daughter, Cinthia Iradukunda, and also to all my children who encouraged me greatly from the beginning of this project, with tender loving kindness, and continued to do so till the completion of this project.

My admonition to any reader reading this, is to be strong in the power of His might; be courageous and wait upon God. Always remember life and death are in our tongues; knowing that the wages of sin is death and that the gift of life from God is in Christ".

The Truth fought for me against spiritual and physical death, and also rescued me through the holy angels of God. Hence, my goal is to let everyone hear and know how to overcome.

I have been called by the Lord God to tell people about my life in Christ Jesus.

The Truth that fought the 1994 genocide against Tutsi still fights and promotes justice. The Truth leads to the confession, and repentance that establishes complete healing to anyone that is willing to embrace the word.

Preface: **Truth that Fights**

Genocide against Tutsi in Rwanda, 1994

"To every man there openeth
A Way, and Ways, and a Way.
And the High Soul climbs the High Way,
And the low Soul gropes the low,
And in between on the misty flats,
The rest drift to and fro.
But to every man there openeth
A High Way and a Low
And every man decideth
The Way his soul shall go".
- Proverb by John Oxenham.

Caught in the web of death; without the right to live, to speak, to eat, to drink, to be loved, and tormented to death- then I was raised to life. I was hopeless, but Heaven fought for me; these all happened in mysterious ways and in the presence of my enemies.

I can truthfully say my entire life today is a testimony of what it means to be saved, guided, led, directed, protected, shielded and nourished by the Word, the Truth. My biological parents, adoptive parents, and spiritual parents, were able to raise me because they stood and clung to this same Word, the Truth. Growing in maturity and confidence in what I had to do with my faith aided me greatly as I arose from the ashes of life, though I had to pass through fire. When the enemy of my life rejoiced that all hope was over, I survived and was raised to life. I am grateful for the Word of the Truth spoken into my life which became the instrument of my rescue to live and tell the tale.

Genocide and the Impact on Humanity

Genocide is the intentional killing of a large amount of people from a particular nation or ethnic group with the sole aim of destroying or wiping out that nation or group of people.

All human right of those who went through it were stripped away, and were inhumanly equated to mere animals, vermin, insects, or diseases. My entire family, friends, and I; were named 'Cockroaches' at the time by most, if not all.

This is also my opportunity to give a first-hand account to all my friends, families, co-workers, and communities who have been constantly probing me to know as well as visit the "land of thousand hills" called Rwanda.

Pre-genocide against Tutsi Rwanda 1994.

After the passing of my grandfather, my grandmother migrated from Bunyambiriri, Nyamagabe to Cyangugu in Rwanda, with a family friend of her late husband. He was a chief in the community. However, he was later stripped off of these functions.

My grandmother was left widowed at an early age with three little children to raise, and lived closely with a family friend of her late husband; a chief leader of the community. There came a time when close friends started to show jealousy towards the children of my grandmother, one of these children was my father. As a young man, my father was regarded to be good looking and very clever in school amongst his peers.

Unfortunately, due to the jealousy, a sinister plan was hatched which involved him to be kidnapped, and taken to some rich people to serve as a domestic worker in Bukavu, Congo-Zaire in 1940. My grandmother was worried as a result of this ill-fated incident, until she stumbled upon the news that revealed the truth. My grandmother continued to care for the remaining children, with hopes to reunite with her son someday.

Rwanda was predominantly made up of the Hutu, Tutsi and

Twa population. There was a time these people all lived together as a very peaceable community. The Tutsis and Hutus were predominantly cattle herdsmen, with large fields for agriculture. These communities mainly depended on the harvests from the farmland. Like everywhere else, the 'Rich and Poor' divide also existed within these kingdoms. However, the Twa population were well known for their hunters and potters.

Prior to the genocide, these populations all lived in harmony, spoke the same language "Kinyarwanda", and shared a vibrant and rich culture- in addition to other social activities. There was mutual respect, and a healthy appreciation for beautiful dances as one of the main expressions of joy in the Rwandan philosophy. They also shared the same opportunities, and there was an availability for all members of the population to access studies out of their comfort zones.

History informs us that Germany colonised Rwanda from 1897 to 1918. The colonization was later handled by Belgium until the 1st of July in 1962. The colonialists found the leadership was previously under a local monarch, which gave room for exploitation through ideological-cum-political interests. This event led to the rise of unrest and violence by the Hutu against Tutsi.

.

What is Rwanda?
Often referred to as "The land of a thousand hills"; Rwanda is a country in East-Central Africa. Officially the Republic of

Rwanda, it is a landlocked country in the Great Lakes region and East Africa converge. Located a few degrees south of the Equator and bordered by Uganda, Tanzania, Burundi, and the Democratic Republic of the Congo. The official languages spoken are Kinyarwanda, French, English. Its capital is Kigali, and its current population is 12,956,000, according to the 2021 census. Unfortunately, there were over 800,000 people slaughtered by the Hutu extremists in just 100 days!

Historically, the commencement of the killings and mutilation of Tutsi people began in 1959. This included burning their houses and mutilating their livestock. "Cut down the tail trees". The weapons used to mutilate and murder people were the machetes which were traditionally designed for weeding and farming activities. This was the principal tool used by both the rich and the poor people in their destructive exercise.

Photo of Machetes (Knives)

The violence was so intense that many Tutsi people fled by finding refuge and shelter in neighbouring countries; mostly in Burundi, Congo (formerly known as Zaire), Tanzania, Uganda, Kenya, and in far Europe, as well as the United States of America and Canada.

The massacre of the Tutsi population was done due to various colonial historical involvement and other political factors that manipulated the Hutu population to hate the Tutsi. Retrospectively, both the Hutu and Tutsi lived together, co-existed and intermarried each other.

In a previous life, there was both the Tutsi farmer and the Hutu farmer. They both shared a communal adversity. The apparent hatred brought silence division and discrimination, creating irreconcilable differences between them through the spread of false ideologies.

The dualism of poverty, and prosperity was on an equal measure with attendant respect for each other.

My parents brought me up to be respectful and obedient. They raised me to never have hatred against anybody, irrespective of skin colour or ethnicity, Hutu or Tutsi, and to always love everyone without any discrimination. This Word of Truth still fights for me till today.

Chapter 1
Death haunted but Truth fought

"Tears are at times as eloquent as words" (Weeping hath a voice)
- Ancient Latin proverb

Death haunted to envelop me with premature death, but Truth fought against all the devices of wickedness over me. In all the tribulations and trials, the spoken words had great impact of rescue and till today, I live a life of favour and mercy to the glory of God.

A: "In-house Operation"

There I was, a frail child, limp and pale, sprawled on a mat in the sun. I had not eaten or drunk for days, yet my entire body was distended like a bag of rotting matter. I became very sick, so my parents gave up on me and laid me down outside in the scorching sun. They were just waiting for me to die; as they had given up hope of ever seeing me alive.

My whole body was bloated due to not having the appropriate treatment. My situation deteriorated by the day, even as they constantly checked to see if I was still breathing.

A passer-by, Sekanyambo, saw me in this critical situation, and he was moved with compassion. He would by no means watch this helpless child die. This stranger, whom I refer to as my God-sent helper, enquired from my parents to find out if he could do something about my health. He later got the consent of my parents to do whatever could be done to save my life.

Hastily, he demanded a blazing hot fire be prepared.

This man kindly asked them to prepare a very hot fire, and brought many herbs; root plants, fresh cow milk and a sharpened knife. He slowly raised the knife into the orange flames, and then mixed all the ingredients in one container. He took the extremely red-hot knife and placed it on my neck at two different places right under my cheek. Yellow fluids gushed out of my neck before I fell limp and transcended into a coma. After which, he made me drink the mixed ingredients of the different herbs, and root plants mashed with cow milk.

No sooner than later, I started to breathe and continued to breathe better as each day passed by. They also continued to feed me with the concoction my helper had made and soon enough, I started gaining strength. Strangely enough, I began to walk but the healing process took much longer than expected for my full recovery. However, the traditional treatment had a significant side effect on me; I developed serious allergies to cow milk and other dairy products.

In retrospect, I will say it was by the grace of God that I am alive today, as I had no control over what they had given me to consume. Besides, the fact that I detest milk to this day, the treatment left me with bold scars. The hot knife of this indigenous treatment left physical and mental scars on my neck that have I grown up with, causing me indignity and shame. I was given a new name, Nyirandegeya (loose skin). This awful nickname resulted in contributing to my low self-esteem, which in effect crushed my confidence, and therefore restricted me from going out to play with my peers; and also led to always wearing a T-shirt to cover up the burn.

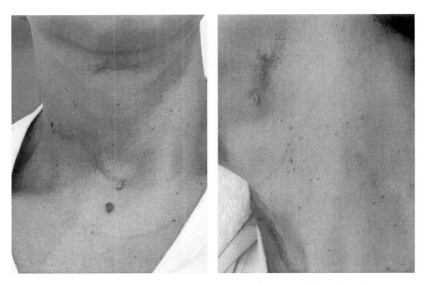

Traces of scars after being operated on with hot knife

My advice here is, do not call children or young people by evil nicknames as these may have adverse effects on their confidence and self-esteem. Handling such pain could become detrimental to their mental health. Thus, leaving them to be extremely vulnerable, mentally scarred for life, and make them suffer in silence.

B. My Farm Experience

After surviving the harrowing in-house operation experience, death was still lurking near. I was five years old playing in the field, when another grave incident missed its target, which was me apparently.

As my mother ploughed the field, I would run to and fro to gain attention playfully. "Slash!" – The sound reverberated in my ears, as the blade wasn't seen but heard. The splatter of blood and piercing pain made it clear- I had been cut! The blood slowly dripped to the ground, as the gaping wound poured.

My mum panicked, and ran away franticly as my father threatened her life telling her if I died, he would see to it that she would also die. But as usual, God's help was nearby. My father swiftly cradled me as I wailed in his arms and he put me onto his back. My foot limply draped as blood dripped, while my face got drastically pale.

The sweat dripped from his brow as he made the two-hour journey to the hospital, as my time was limited. Thankfully, I made it to the hospital. Till this day, I am unsure how I survived such a dire circumstance. The brazen scar on my left foot is a constant reminder of God's grace. Eventually, my mother returned to the family and my parents were reconciled by the fact her mistake was not deadly.

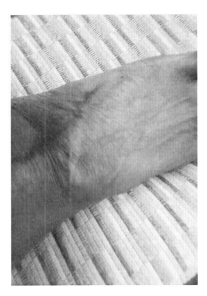

Left foot nearly got chopped off in my childhood

C. The Heated Gathering

From that time, my grandmother raised me in Rwanda while my parents lived in Congo. As a child, I didn't know or understand the political propaganda against us, so I played blissfully with other kids. Unknown to me, we were sacrificed yearly.

Annually, houses and farms were set ablaze, along with corpses. The media only heightened this conflict with propaganda splattered in the media like innocent blood. It was surely enough to groom an entire generation of extremists who were prepared to kill!

My grandmother loved Rwanda but she was blinded to the cracks in her nation. She was not alone, many others stood in a deadly relationship with our nation. The atrocities continued to brew from 1959-1990, until they began overspilling.

I vividly recall one night in 1962, a friend invited us to share the cultural harvest of wine products. We were jousting with glee when panic suddenly struck. Fumes filled the air, as our house was set on fire. We could only imagine what would have become of us if we were asleep. Needless to say, God saved us from the burning fire.

D. Pacing the Border

For a year, we briefly stayed in a family friend's compound, who was a friend indeed. This very man informed us about the ploy to destroy our lives. Swiftly, my grandmother clothed me in double layers, with money neatly stashed in the folds of my clothes. I was warned to keep it a secret till I arrived at my other grandmother's side at a nearby village.

That night, she trudged through the bush amidst the nightly hoots of the night crawlers, and across banana fields; where serpents laid waiting. Somehow, I think she knew the rattling snake was a better companion than the terrorists that hunted us — Hutu.

How could man fear their fellow men more than the beast of the field? Luckily, she arrived at a nearby village where I was left in the safety of another family.

The Hutu killers searched for us at our former dwelling but they couldn't find us. We were long gone, and our secret was safe with our landlord.

I was weary of my surroundings and longed for my grandmother's presence, because it had all happened so fast. One moment we were together as a perfect family, and the next we weren't.

Once grandmother returned, we journeyed toward Bukavu. Bukavu is a city in Eastern Democratic Republic of Congo.

There, we spent one week at the border. As a child, this all seemed puzzling to me. My life depended on her, but at that moment, I believe she was as vulnerable as a little child. I looked up to her, as she looked up to God.

The day was very long and gruelling. By this time, grandmother had grown tired of my despondence, and had begun scolding me until I broke down in uncontrollable sobs. The day turned into night, and I had given up hope as my sobs subsided, and my heavy lids closed. Just then, the entire house let out a startling roar- She had arrived!

Our family were in tears at her arrival, as they were previously told she had been killed. "No Tutsi can cross the border! How did you do it?", My father cried. She began to relay the story of how she disguised herself with a bunch of bananas on her head as an exporting saleswoman. The moment she found the security guards were distracted, she crossed over.

In my mind, I only feared losing her, whilst she feared the loss of our lives.

E. Brave Childhood

In 1969, the Congolese authorities began to conspire with the Rwanda Authorities. This majorly had to do with Tutsi refugees in Bukavu. The plot here involved repatriation of the Tutsi refugees back to Rwanda. The politics behind this was to eventually kill them, as they were viewed as 'Cockroaches'. We listened ardently to the news, eager to make sense of the atmosphere, and just like that, Congo was transformed from a haven to a mine field.

My father didn't have the option to hide since he was forced to provide for our extended family. Therefore, he continued to work. He was known as an upstanding, and intelligent man within the community. These were the type of men the government desired to humiliate. Without any notice, on a random day, my father did not come home. Though we did not know where he was, our fears revealed the truth.

I was 13 years old. I sat in the dark room as I observed my mother distressed. She wept woefully. "Let me look for him, mama...", I gently told her. Once she agreed, I bravely ran to his employer. There I realised our worst fear, as Father's boss relayed the devastating message. My father was arrested, deported, and incarcerated from his place of employment.

Moved with compassion, the manager gave me a letter to take to the prison. I went, and I found my dad in detention. He looked so unfamiliar to me as he sat despairingly in the cell. What a contrast this was to his usual macho character! Tears stung my eyes as I handed the letter to the authority. I was unaware of the content of the letter but shortly after, he was released and sent to the local village called Shangi Changugu in Rwanda.

After returning with the good news, my mum started to send me regularly. With each visit, my father reassured me with the hope of a reunion, and I so believed him. He was strong and wise. I admired him greatly for these attributes.

Eventually, as I had hoped, my father escaped and fled from the village! Once again, our home was filled with unspeakable joy and relief. My mother was elated and revived by his arrival.

From then on, I was given a new rank in the home. My new responsibility was to send urgent messages to our relatives that were left behind. Though we knew not how long we'd be secure, I knew I would no longer play the role of a bystander.

F. Survivor of War Schramme-Mulele

Pierre Mulele was a Congolese active rebel, and former Minister of Education in Patrice Lumumba's Cabinet. After the assassination of Lumumba, Mulele became one of the top Lumumbists fighting against the government in power.

Lumumba Patrice was a politician and independent leader, who served as the first prime minister of the Democratic of the Congo. He was assassinated on 17th January, 1961.

Jean Schramme was a Belgian mercenary for Mulele, who began war in Bukavu in 1967. He launched surprise attacks on Bukavu.

During the horrible war of Schramme in RDC (Republic Democratic of Congo), we faced challenges in refugee places due to the absence of water, food, and firewood. My young sister and I were the only children that could go out searching for food, wood, and water. This was because my older teenage sisters were at a higher risk of being raped by soldiers.

Regardless of my age, I helped sell firewood, coals, and local flour made at the market street called Limanga/Bukavu. My sister and I would travel miles daily to fetch water. I carried these responsibilities in an addition to my studies in school, which I excelled at.

During this time in Congo, a wealthy family member wanted to adopt two young children (relatives), who at the time were living in Rwanda. Knowing my level of maturity, my parents selected me to relay this message to help bring the children across the border. I figured it was a sense of duty, and I was honoured for the recommendation. I went off with the mission to a village called Ibiguzi/Changugu in Rwanda. Since I was a young child, I was allowed to travel more freely, unlike the adults who were Tutsi.

I walked directly to Rwanda without ceasing, until I reached my destination. I arrived on the same day, despite running under the heat of the tropical sun. When I arrived and relayed this message, the family was reluctant to let the boy and girl come back with me to Congo. In spite of this, I managed to convince them by asserting them they would be in good hands.

I left a good impression on them, and they agreed for us to make the journey back to Congo. We made our journey back that same day, running home and not looking back. I was fortunate to accomplish whatever I needed in my childhood to make my parents and grandmother happy. I am grateful they gave me excellent manners and education.

Do not to despise children of any age. These children are your stepping hill in many circumstances. Do not stop them from doing work, instead encourage them and give them responsibilities.

Every human is created to do good work, no matter the age. I believe in giving children opportunities, so their talents are not wasted. My belief is that, had I not been equipped with these skills, I would not be the courageous woman that I am today. I wonder, if I did not have the kind of exposure I had in my childhood, would I have been able to withstand the challenges that came?

G. Unstoppable

A few years later, I had evolved into a mature teen and I finished high school, but I couldn't find a college nearby. Desperate for admission, I implored my parents to allow me to seek out another school. However, these colleges were Catholic missionary schools in remote villages, but I had a plan.

Early the next morning, I ventured into the town centre in search of a lorry. The sun beat down my neck and back as I waved for the vehicles to stop. I was relieved when a rusty, dirt-cladded chariot halted. I mounted the truck and held firmly to the sides as it took its jagged journey to the province. My heart beamed with joy and excitement as I swayed to and fro. This was my chance!

My spirit leapt, but my body drooped in the African heat until the truck stopped in front of a school. I didn't remember looking at the driver whilst I bid farewell, for I was enamoured by the neat establishment with modern finishing that laid before me. Though I casually walked to the registration office, it felt as though I had run.

"I am here to register for college!", I stated gladly. The sister in front of the counter paused and stared at me, puzzled. "Registration closed two weeks ago." She replied me and my heart dropped. The enormity of the day minced with the excitement of the possibility had now turned to despair.

I sluggishly treaded to the main road to find transportation back. The road was quiet and still; dust danced under the pedestrians' feet, but not a single truck was in sight. I was thirsty, hungry and anguished, and so was the sun as it slowly turned away.

Not sure what to do next, I stared at each civilian and noticed a woman walking in my direction. She kindly offered a room for the night. It was clear this was the only option I had left for the day.

That night I laid awake, alert to every sound, mortal and immortal, until day broke. When morning finally came, I was eager to continue my journey to familiarity. This journey would be so like many others, but I was determined not to give up; neither did my parents, just to demonstrate the intensity of their support.

After enduring the difficult search, I found a college and I was admitted to study in a boarding school college at Katana/ Mwanza. Of course, I was ecstatic but somehow within me, I knew that this struggle was another injustice I faced due to my nationality. Out of all the college doors I knocked on, why was I only accepted where the Head staff was Rwandan? Somehow, I knew that was the beginning of my fight.

The experience trained my offspring. When my daughter was 8 years old, there was a time she was separated from me. In this time, I got an opportunity for her to join me. The distance of separation was so wide and many miles to reach to me.

I remember telling her to be brave, courageous, and for her to tell God she wanted to join her mum. I reassured her that she was sin-free therefore God was listening to her prayer.

Bravely and courageously, my child talked to God and spoke to Him in prayer, "My God, take me to my mum". She travelled a long way and joined me peaceably without any cost. There are times God uses a divine help to support us for His own glory. I am challenging everyone to build children in a brave manner, not to relent in their ability. God hearkens to the voice of the children with fruitful results because they offer sacrifices of honest and innocent aroma unto God.

The power of your tongue has life in line with God's will. In watching and observing all these dramatic situations, my desire to become a strong woman in the future was more strengthened.

Chapter 2
From Hopelessness to Hope

"No matter the direction of the wind, the sun is always where it should go."

Young people must be trained for a better future; no matter their state of living. A good or bad environment can lift up, or destroy a child.

Living with Mice, iznsects and intestinal worms

For most of my childhood, I was brought up by my grandmother as a refugee, and I eagerly listened to every detail of her counselling. Our category of accommodation was the lowest habitation named Nyamugo/Bukavu in the Republic Democratic of Congo (former Congo Zaire). This did not affect us as I was a very joyful and happy refugee young girl. There was no electricity, sharing of public water tap, no transportation, no shoes, no clothes. However, she inculcated in me the beauty of morals and values in becoming a greater person.

I used to spend some time with my parents in the daytime, then go to stay with my grandmother. She was making sure I went to school, and did my homework before night. One of the important lessons she gave me which impacted my studies and prepared me to be a good future wife was, "My daughter, you shall never have sexual contact with any man before your marriage." She said again, "You must study and get your qualification diploma, and afterwards, the man to be your future husband will locate you."

The conditions and environment of my studies were not easy. I revised only during the daytime, and then would go to bed as soon as it turned dark. The state of our house as refugees was very bad, to the extent of having no toilet inside the house.

There were so many mice everywhere both on the outside and inside, so I slept covering up my head. Alas, each time I woke up in the morning, I would find many bitemarks left by mice on my feet, and their faeces around my sleeping place; especially around my feet. The skin of my feet was eaten by mice, but that did not deter my focus and determination.

The spots left by mosquito bites on my face was clearly feasible and evident. This could also be seen on my clothes, and blankets that had holes by the rat and mice.

I had chronic stomach pain every day; I was constantly vomiting intestinal worms and also excreting worms. My grandmother would give me traditional herbal medicine to ingest, but it was never effective. I lived in that condition and whenever, I felt something coming out my throat, I would go to hide to vomit, or would put my finger down my throat to make myself throw up the worms.

Have you been in such a state in life where you just take all that is being thrown at you, and can only focus on what will be tomorrow?

The mice excreta were everywhere but I had no choice. We lived this way until the Lord rescued me, and changed my level of living. Though I lived a tough life, I had in my mind that I must succeed in my studies.

You may be living today in a place of discomfort, but I can tell you there is a way out to reach your destiny. God saves His people and turns their lives into living testimonies to encourage others. You just have to key to the following points:

Wipe Off Tears

"No one can beat you if you fight for the truth" - Sourabh Kumar

My life was full of challenges, but in all, I came out victorious. In my youth, I went to look for a better life, but was forced and coerced into joining the army services. From the beginning, I found myself lost in a big, foreign town without any family. It was a nightmare! I could not cry or smile; I was mute with a burning in my heart. I was restless and constantly thought of running away.

I was hopeless but God made a way for me. The true Fight, aligned with the will of God, lifted a compatriot to me for help.

After a while, I met a girl and we became friends. She introduced me to her uncle; he was a person with wisdom and understanding, I seized the opportunity to embrace his hospitality as him and his wife kindly agreed for me to live with them for some time, whilst I figured out my journey and education.

How did I escape? One day, I put on my own clothes and covered it up with my uniform. I walked through the bushes, sat down, took off the uniform and threw them away. Then, I took the bus and praise be to God, I arrived at my friend's family house.

I had the vision to study to become a strong woman in future. This family raised me, restored, and accepted me into their home. I was fully dependant on them for all my needs, support, and my safety. They took care of me and registered me into college, and later in university.

As they trained me and encouraged me to study, they also warned me to be careful to avoid any sexual shenanigans. The father advised me, "My daughter, do not trust any man right

now. You must protect yourself against any sexual temptation."
He said, "I know your biological father, a noble man of integrity.
I don't want Him to hear that you have been sexually abused
while living with us".

I took the advice and pursued my studies at the University
Level and obtained a Bachelor's Degree in Chemistry and
Biology. The counselling and moral values received both from
my biological parents, and my adoptive parents trained me to
be excellent.

After my graduation, many bachelors desired my courtship.
However, the ball was in my court to choose the best one of
them all, and I fell in love with the most handsome, educated,
and kindest man — Joseph Nyagatare.

The pestilences are around to bite you because you have a great
destiny. The Grace of God is lifting us up from the pestilences
to be the source of benediction.

The Bible says, "Train up your children the way they should
go, for when they grow, they will not depart from it (Proverbs
22:6)". When you are training your children, you are investing
into their life, and in tribulation they will remember to fight and
win the battle.

I kept all the advice and warnings from my young age. I loved
myself and loved looking forward to a good future, with an

intense focus to be respectful and dignified.

My tears were wiped off when I met compassionate and merciful people. What can we learn from this?

- Open the doors to your house. Be kind to the people in need. Make sacrifices to offer hospitality to others, and wipe away their tears knowing that someone is bleeding and looking where to go, but you can be an answer at that moment.

- Have the heart of compassion and God will fight for you, for He will never leave us nor forsake us. Give out your best and it shall come back to you.

- You are the divine helper nominated to feed, or to accommodate, or to cloth a hopeless person.

- You are gifted and talented, so be productive while you are on this earthly planet.

My adoptive father and his wife have become the blessed ones because of their hospitality to others in need. The works they did in my life are evidence of good and selfless works.

Truth Destroyed the Plan to Rape

Some years ago, our parents warned us to be careful as we moved around in the society. Our culture was that if a girl had sexual relations with any man before marriage, the girl would be rejected, thereby making the girl a disgrace to her family. My grandmother told me many years ago, if a girl became pregnant and the man rejected her, the family would ostracise her to an island and she would be abandoned to be picked up by unknown people living on the island. Today, I encourage all to fight a good fight to protect your children, and all young people that can be exposed to sexual abuse.

My First Encounter: Travelling

I was sent by my mum from Bukavu, Congo (RDC) to Cyangugu, Rwanda. On my way back, the soldiers stopped my young sister and I, at the border. They took us off the roadside and went near the bushes. For some reason, I got a clue these men wanted to rape us.

I started to plead with them straightaway. I pled for them to have mercy on us and for them to release us to go home. They just stared at me and after a while, they released us. I followed the advice of my parents, in addition with the grace of God that was upon me. Do not be a prey to the devil, and as a matter of principle; activate your faith, your value and your morals through your actions.

My Second Encounter: At Home

At some point, my parents hosted one of my family members

in our home. One day, my parents left me at home and there I was babysitting. He decided to come closer to me, and sought to touch me. I raised my voice and told him not to try it. He knew no one could hear as we were home alone.

He kept following me around the home, and when I noticed, he was unwilling to yield, I ran downstairs, took a sharp knife, and aggressively pointed it at him.

I was screaming and shouting for him to leave me, and the Truth fought for me and abolished his plan to rape me. This inspiration to defend myself was heaven sent, and it was all I needed to defeat the Devil who knew my destiny was great. God does not want us to be abused because He acknowledges our body is precious and honourable.

My Third Encounter: Visiting a Friend

My goal was always to protect my body against any sexual immorality till I found the right man to marry me.

My colleague at work invited me to his house just after service. Immediately I entered his house, he locked the door and hid the key, then said, "From now, you are now my wife." I was overwhelmed with fear, but I calmed down and confidently tried to figure out how I could escape.

He knew I was engaged to another man, but he was planning on raping me. It was a common thing in those days that if a man kidnapped a girl for a night, the culture would demand she be condemned to stay with him as his wife. No other man could marry a girl that was victim of rape; regardless of the circumstances that led to the rape. The news would be spread all over, and it would destroy the lady's reputation in the society. She would be rejected and ashamed, even by her own parents and relatives who were already expecting to have a good son-in-law in future, who would pay her dowry.

I pretended to be nice and respectful to him. I kept responding to him nicely and reassured him that we would have to plan a proper wedding.

My heart was beating fast, as I was looking for a good opportunity to trick him in order to escape. After many hours, he fell for my trick, opened the doors to his house, and I was released. However, he did not give up on me and attempted to kill me on several occasions.

When his evil plan to kill me was discovered, the police arrested him and exiled him into another city far away from where I was. He was given a restraining order and was told not to ever come near me again, otherwise he would end up in jail. Be careful even of your own colleagues. Also, do not be exposed to the temptations of sexual desire.

My fiancé at the time, Joseph Nyagatare, was informed of what had transpired. He instantly came to help me move, as he lived in a different district. He found me a job at his workplace as a teacher in the same college.

My tongue saved and rescued me from the wrong marriage. The evil my colleague had planned out for me did not end the way he wanted it to.

The truth stands always with the will of God. "Wisdom comes in the middle of troubles and leads to victory".

My Fourth Encounter: Wrong Friendship

My youth was targeted to be destroyed, but God always saved me at the nick of time, as I learned quickly to find ways to rescue myself out of deadly situations. The key is to have emotional intelligence, and also by learning to anticipate people's behaviours.

I used to be friendly with a specific young man, who I met on the road while I was on my way home after class. One day, as I made my way back from college through my usual route, he invited me to come into his family home. As soon as I entered, the atmosphere changed, and he immediately proceeded to rape me.

It was such a big struggle to break free from him, but I eventually managed to escape before he could touch me. From that time on, I learned never to enter the house of a man, even if he was in the family home.

I would encourage everyone to tell the young ones never to accept any invitation from a man or a woman when they are alone. The devil can use the circumstance to take away their virginity. It is crucial to protect children, and to inform them about the dangers that could come from some seemingly innocent invitations from inconspicuous individuals.

My Fifth Encounter: The Home Teacher

My adoptive parents travelled for a work mission, and left me with their family friends. When I was with the family, a gentle and friendly young man offered to help me revise after school. I was so happy and considered him as my own brother- so I allowed him to teach me Maths, French and Sciences, as I was very passionate about my studies.

One day, he suggested for us to go for a walk. As we walked, we went past a quiet environment. At that point, he said to me, "Let us sit down and rest a bit under the tree."

Surprisingly enough, this man started to caress me. I was so stunned, but I refused to allow him caress me. It ensued in a tussle, but he failed to rape me. How did I overcome? By the grace of God —God's grace emboldened me, and it made me so strong.

As I was a stranger in that family, I did not tell anybody about what had happened when I got back to the house. I held on to the secret and was burning with sadness and anger, until I went back to my spiritual parents.

Dear parents and guardians of children, I was preserved to tell others we should train our children, and let them know what lies in their paths, in terms of sexual abuse and practice. Let them be aware of the dangers out there. Teach them to never give up taking care of their body, soul and spirit.

I kept silent and never shared my challenges. None of my near-rape encounters were discussed with anyone.

Now that I'm all grown and able to speak out, I have made it my mission to bring it to the knowledge of everyone, so that people can understand and educate against the horrible things young people face.

My desire is to warn parents or guardians, and carers — to know what can happen when a youth or child of any age is left unattended to. Youths are so attractive to the devil. As a survivor from many attempts of rape, I live to tell my story and I want to remind nations and generations, to protect young people against any attempt of rape.

At an early stage of my life, I became a widow in 1994, but I made the decision to pursue my goals and to hold on to the vows I had made to God Almighty. As a single widowed parent, it was not easy to raise my children, but I had firm and strict rules in my household to protect them from any attempt and harm.

I stripped away any form of pride from myself and always put their wellbeing first. I would lay down my life for them, to ensure their safety.

When any of my daughters took a liking and passion for any activity, I would spend my evenings accompanying them to ensure their safety. On many occasions, I would go the extra mile of bringing them food at their university library during those crunch hours of deadlines and revisions, then I would go back later to pick them up. This not only encouraged them, but also made them know I was rooting for them to succeed. Fundamentally, it protected them from harm, and gave them the confidence and boost they needed at the time.

These are the small things we do as parents to create a space, where our children can thrive safely. I recall a time when one of my daughters, was much younger and actively involved in the church choir at Arise and Shine Christian Ministries in Manchester, United Kingdom. Each Saturday at her choir rehearsals, I would support her by taking her there, and quietly lying down in the car until the rehearsal was finished.

All of this, I did to offer the best possible experience for the education and achievements of all my children. When we can, we must guide them through the possible dangers of all kinds of environments. We must take time to teach them the realities of the world. We must consider elements such as their mode of transport, and when possible- we must endeavour to facilitate their movement between the home and the destination of any of their programs or activities.

I encourage you to use discernment when making the decision to leave your young children for long hours away from your supervision, as you are their main confidant and gatekeeper.

Support and encourage them to be with people of great virtue. When left alone, they become vulnerable to the intent of the enemy, which is to devour their chastity and to steal their destiny. I am a living testimony; I have been saved and rescued to tell all generations and nations of my experiences. The Truth that Fights the enemy of our destiny is our tongue, our mouth, and the Word in our hearts.

We shall plant good seeds in the lives of younger generations, in order to prepare them for their future, and when they do become mature, our children can choose to live victoriously and prosperously in society.

Chapter 3
The Holocaust

"Rain beats the leopard's skin, but it does not wash out the spots"

A.   Genocide in Rwanda, 1994: Tutsi Dehumanised Like Cockroaches

From 1959 to 1994, the government in power developed a propaganda for killing Tutsi people; burning their houses, and killing all their cattle. Yet, there were no investigations carried out into the criminal acts on the innocent population. There was no right of protection for minority groups, because it was the desire of government in power to wipe out the population of Tutsi population. The segregation was so strong that all documents had to show tribal identification, even on school certificates (Hutu, Tutsi or Twa) as this was the only way to tell them apart.

The Tutsi could only study to primary school level, after this there were severe restrictions placed against them to further their education, either at high school, or at the college/university.

Life became so difficult that a Tutsi man or woman would be insulted for merely passing by. The expected response was to keep quiet without retaliation.

In my adulthood, I moved to Burundi where I got married to my husband, Joseph. We lived there for some time as refugees. Soon enough, my late husband became tired of remaining in that kind of life in Burundi. He made the decision for us to return to his homeland.

In 1986, we moved to Rwanda to be closer to my husband's family. Many young Tutsi's were denied the access to basic and University education, or even the simple opportunity to go to college with their ID Ethnicity document.

Each time I got arrested, I denied being a Rwandan citizen and argued aggressively against the fact, with the hope of not being harmed if they realised the truth of my ethnicity. Whenever I visited my parents, I refused to take a Rwandan ID to avoid being obstructed. I kept my Congolese ID and luckily enough, it saved me later during the genocide.

By October in 1990, the Rwandan Patriotic Front finally opted to deliver Rwandan citizens from the horrible discriminatory killing of the Tutsi. I was arrested and detained during the period. However, I was later released when I declared I was not a Rwandan citizen.

During my stay in Rwanda with my late husband, Joseph Nyagatare, we lived in a socially insecure and volatile atmosphere. We were forced to accept the conditions of the societal inequalities then. Throughout this time, Joseph was the headmaster of the Local High school and College, and I taught biological sciences at the same institute.

Joseph was a man of wisdom and integrity, and acted as a peacemaker towards everyone he encountered. He was loved by all his students and showed no discrimination. This private school became a reliable school as he fought for the best interests of all students and staff. Numerous parents from different provinces, and backgrounds sent their young boys and girls to study at this institution.

It didn't take long till the school authorities, and some government officials began to disseminate false information against him. They instigated discriminatory allegations against him by saying he was an Inyenzi (cockroach). All students, and most of the teachers refrained from plotting against him. They rallied around him and supported him.

We loved all students, and fought for their interests and benefits, preparing them for a promising future without reference to their racial, or economical background. Friends advised Joseph to give up and flee the country because of the persecution he received, but he refused for the sake of the students and his love for his homeland.

I can imagine many people would like to know what I mean by 'Holocaust' and how it applied to a particular group of people living in Rwanda from April, 1994 to 4th of July, 1994.

A holocaust is a great (or complete) devastation or destruction; especially by fire or heat. It can also be described as the deliberate killing of a large number of people from a particular nation, or ethnic group with the sole aim of completely destroying that nation or group.

During the Rwandan genocide against Tutsi in April 1994, all human rights of the Tutsi population were radically stripped away. The entire Tutsi population were equated to animals, vermin, insects, or diseases. For example, the Nazis referred to Jews as 'Vermin' and similarly during the genocide, the Tutsi population were referred to as cockroaches, 'Inyenzi' in the Kinyarwanda language.

In this stage, the hate propaganda in print and on radio were used to vilify the victim group. Interahamwe (government trained youths) were systematically raised to kill the Tutsis and moderate Hutus who were against the animosity. The Interahamwe were authorised to carry all types of swords, guns, explosive bombs, armoured vehicles, machetes, primitive hammers, and wooden sticks. They premeditatively killed an estimated number of 800,000 to 1,000,000 within 100 days; this ultimately led to the mass slaughter of the Tutsi population.

The government in power used all its propaganda machinery to spread bigotry and hatred for the Tutsi population. Men, women, and children were no longer recognised as human but referred to as cockroaches. Lists were compiled of those who were marked out as targets, and were then assassinated in horrific ways. This was a systematic way of destroying this ethnic group. We were informed by one individual, who was aware of this that my husband was on the top of the list. He was warning us to remain vigilant and find a way to escape.

They made up misleading accusations against him, saying our house would be the meeting place of the Inyenzis (the cockroaches) on 1st of Feb, 1994. When this date arrived, our neighbours secretly came to see if the meeting was taking place. All this propaganda began to be published on the RTLM Radio (Radio Television Libre de Mille), illustrating the weight of their hate through media. All our friends, and everyone who knew the truth were speechless about the insidious, and highly lethal claims that were being spread through the media.

RTLM Collines was a Rwandan radio station that started broadcasting in 1993, and was influential for disseminating hatred against Tutsis. The mutilation of Tutsi had started sporadically all over the country, yet there was no further investigation as to their fundamental human rights. This made us even more frightened and we decided to flee with our older children to a neighbouring country called Burundi.

We did not have any voice or defence in all of this because the authorities had established hit lists everywhere for those they were supposed to kill, before carrying out the mass exterminations. The list comprised of all educated Tutsis; business families, farmers, workers, men, and women. A sympathetic Hutu came to warn us that we were on top of the list, as I was a teacher in a private College, ACEJ Karama School District Muhanga, Southern Province, Rwanda, and my husband was also headmaster at the school. In spite of all these occurrences, my husband refused to abandon the students.

Tutsi dehumanised as cockroaches

B. My Restlessness

The 6th of April, 1994 was the official beginning of the genocide and calamity for all the Tutsi population.

It was truly the holocaust for all the Tutsi population. Even though a list existed consisting of the major Tutsi players to be eliminated, everyone else had now become a target for slaughter. Thousands of people had no way to escape or hide.

This act frightened the entire nation, especially the Tutsi – up to the extent that even the reasonable Hutus were frightened to give shelter to a fellow Tutsi. The contrasting physical attributes used to differentiate a Tutsi from a Hutu were attributes such as the appearance of the nose; broad or slim lines, stature, height and light skin tones. These features sometimes made a person with the aforementioned attributes a clear target and a victim.

The government declared a lockdown and ordered the hunting of all Tutsi with the intent to kill them all over the country. This was done with the aid of machetes, guns and swords. These tools were already in storage and were then distributed to the Hutu population who were partakers in the extermination. Only the génocidaires (Rwandans guilty of genocide) moved about freely, killing every Tutsi in every location. Dozens of women, men, children, pregnant women, disabled, blind, and babies were killed.

Machetes, knives, heavy hammers, and grenades, were distributed by the authorities to kill the Tutsis. Most of the Tutsi population were either stabbed, or mutilated, or even beaten to death with wooden sticks. A person was deemed fortunate to be killed by a gunshot, as extreme killers decided not to waste bullets; but found it rather more productive to use a machete instead. In some places, the killers supervised their young children in beating Tutsis to death.

I hid everywhere I could, looking for refuge —even in the ravine of bushes, but I could never find a safe place. Neighbours isolated us, watching us through their windows and compound.

On one occasion, the presidential bodyguards' soldiers came to our main road searching for my husband. A good neighbour lied to them that he did not live in the area. He then went to hide in the nearest village.

I also ran to the local mosque to bring out our late friend, Malakiya, who at the time was the head of the Islamic population and our family friend, so he could hide also. He was a very influential man in the community and a Tutsi, so he was endangered.

I took another direction to find a secure place. I ran to a friend, then met a driver of a lorry with other refugees, and headed to Butare with them (in the Southern province of Rwanda, second town of Rwanda back in the day). The journey lasted about two hours. As the distance between Butare to Muhanga is 101km (62.758 miles) by road.

When I fled to Butare, I left the little children at home with the maid servants to keep them safe, as I thought the main targets were adults. I figured if I was not with them, they would be safe. However, I did not know that innocent children were also being slaughtered.

On April 19, 1994 in Butare, I did not have any money, and thus had to exchange my expensive watch with someone for a ticket to pay the pick-up driver as I was running for my life. I stayed a week in a village district called Rusatira, before I became restless and fearful. I knew I had to find a way to return to my hometown to see my little children.

Unknown to me, Butare had become a central massacre zone. God was leading me out to rescue me and once I left, they killed everyone in that village.

A driver passed by with passengers and agreed to take me to where they were heading to. He was laughing ironically and saying: "I don't know if you will arrive there safely." He jokingly spoke about what I had left behind in the town of Butare, not knowing that most of Tutsi were already killed in Butare town.

He said in a very sarcastic way, "I don't know if you will cross many roadblocks all over the place". Then I convinced him that

I was not a Rwandan citizen and I had no problem. Right then was when I had revelation to camouflage and survive.

Three miles from my home, the soldiers and Interahamwe (Génocidaires) pulled up on the car at the roadblock closer to a bush, which was designed to be a killing site. They were all equipped with guns, machetes, grenades, and hammers in their hands, I could tell they were excited they had gotten me as a prey. They quickly attempted to kill me, but I denied being a Tutsi. My gestures, and body language were enough to blind them. I told them with a confident smile that I was not a Rwandan. They looked at me furiously, and then released the driver to go ahead, so I arrived home.

I found my husband had returned from hiding in the village and decided to come back home to await his final demise.

Murambi was a modern centre and temporary stay for high-ranking members of government who ran away from Kigali-the capital city, to organise and monitor the genocide against the Tutsi population. A friend's driver from the government authorities came from the Cabinet Assembly in Murambi/ Muhanga, and told us about the plan to kill us first.

Frightened by the information, I remained confident that I would live and not die. Before the genocide I had asked my husband to baptise the children, because I knew we needed to be ready, just in case we died during the entire fight – at least

I would know my children would rest peacefully in heaven. Joseph knowing, he was a target would at times say" Oh my God, I hope they shoot me with a gun and let me be killed with the machetes and swords."

On 23rd April, 1994, I spent the night in the bushes with three small children. How did I manage? My neighbour came in the evening, warning us that bodyguards were out on the back street looking to come into our house.

I took my little children and ran to a friend, a member of the parliament, and begged her to hide us but she refused. She told me that the government had given them a letter, warning them not to hide or keep any Tutsi.

Though she was my friend, she refused me entry into her house and told me, "Hide in the bush, behind the pig's shelter". It was both a horrible and an astonishing revelation, but God was in control.

I walked into the bushes at night, and suddenly a man with a machete arrived and nearly slaughtered me. I screamed, "Please have mercy, do not kill me". He was a security guard and recognised me. Just then, I knew God was trying to protect me. The guy said to me, "They have been coming to hunt Tutsi at night to kill". He continued, "If they come, I will cough as a sign that they are around".

I stayed awake all night waiting for the coughing signal. That night, there was a massive slaughter of Tutsis within 500 meters of my home. I heard explosions of heavy machine guns shooting, revolting sounds from grenades, and bombs exploding with a lot of noise and people screaming. Indeed, it was horrible!

Morning arrived, and I walked out from the bushes to my house. A faithful Christian Hutu came to disclose to us what had happened in the night. Many of my friends were killed and thrown in the same hole or mass grave, though some were still alive.

We thank God, one of them, Madam of late Ndushabandi Cassian, was found in the commune pit hole with many dead bodies. She was wounded badly with a knife-machete wound on her neck. Miraculously, she was still breathing and was rescued back to life.

My husband looked at me while he was reading the Bible and said, "My darling, do not run again into bushes". He told me, 'Sit down, let us be killed, and we will go to Heaven to God'.

He said, "I prayed that none of us will be slaughtered, but be shot with a gun". I answered with confidence that I was not going to be killed; I declared that I would live to take care of my children. I was exhausted and had tried all means to run away from this nightmare. There were dead bodies everywhere, around the wayside of road rocks.

Joseph was ready before God, and said, "Anyway, do not worry; the truth will win. We are innocent, and heaven will welcome us". There is power in our tongue; till today, I respect and remember the last conversation I had with him. He said "If I die, please look after my children".

C. Tormented

God always sends to us a divine helper in hopeless situations; to direct and rescue people.

In the early morning on 24th April, 1994, a young man called Damascene, whom I would call a faithful friend and a member of my charismatic prayer group, came and announced to us about the many dead bodies thrown all in the same pit. He discovered some people were thrown alive. We recognised some refugees who came to hide in hotel Concorde/Muhanga.

He told us the plan was to destroy the remaining untouched portion of our area with heavy machine guns and tractors, to kill the remainder of us in Nyabisindu. The cooked-up propaganda against us said our area was full of dehumanized cockroaches and they would have to use heavy machine guns to eliminate each of us.

He brought the late priest, Juvenal of the Catholic Church, Muhanga - and took us in a car, lying down in the backseat.

He drove us to the parish in Kabgayi, a big Christian centre with a cathedral, large school premises and a big hospital. Kabgayi is in the South of Gitarama District, now called Muhanga, and historically Pope John Paul II visited it in September, 1990.

The late priest, Juvenal of Catholic Church (Muhanga), left us within the premises at the entrance of the chapel in respect to the Sunday service, and handed the message to his colleague to hide us. After the mass, the priest seminar school headmaster came and told us to leave the place immediately.

I begged him to hide us and said: 'Have mercy, excellent one'. Instead, He harassed me and terrified us, sarcastically saying, "Why are you here? What are you hiding for?"

"Unless you want a bullet, get out from here quickly.", He replied us with a dirty look on his face.

Suddenly the soldier's bodyguards at the gate heard his words and pointed their guns at us, prepared to shoot. We went outside quickly from the premises and walked on the main road of Kabgayi.

This gate was secured by the bodyguard of soldiers sent from the hostile government against Tutsi.

Everything works together for our good. The word of God says in Romans 8: 28, "And we know that all things work together for our good to those who are called according to His purposes" (KJV).

Seminary Young School a.k.a Petit Seminaire, St. Leon, Kabgayi

Few days after, it came to my knowledge that the génocidaires killed all the Tutsi people who were there, leaving Hutu refugees. I was greatly astonished, because I had previously asked myself why I was rejected and thrown out of the holy place. Yet, I realised the Lord God did not want me to perish; I was pushed outside the premises for my good.

My friend and I, with our children, found ourselves walking outside of the Cathedral in Kabgayi, and we met a lot of Tutsi people from different places looking for a hiding place as well. A Senior Bishop had given an order not to allow any refugees to enter into the Kabgayi Cathedral. He said, "I don't want my

Cathedral to be destroyed." God's grace and mercy literally rained on us that day, and we were then allowed to enter the Cathedral.

My Entrance in Cathedral Kabgayi

I sat down on the floor, not knowing what to do. Fortunately for me, a man who knew my late husband came and moved us into the premises of Saint Joseph College. A College led by Religious Brothers called "Marist and Religious Community". The man who came to move us was one of the religious brothers called Brother Fidele Murekezi. Sadly, he was also killed as a victim of the genocide.

We were many seeking refuge with no food, drink, or cover. We all laid with our mouths shut and our eyes widely opened, waiting for death. Children could not cry, for fear took over in our midst. Many people died starving, and many were slaughtered. The so-called Inyenzis (cockroaches), were dehumanized to die.

Chapter 4
Hiding Grief, No Drop of Tears.

My tears must stop, for every drop hinders needle and thread.
- Proverb by Thomas Hood

On the 25th of April in 1994, the Génocidaires (Interahamwe) killed a hero, my wonderful husband, Joseph Nyagatare. A good friend advised him to hide in a pit disguised as a toilet but he refused saying, "If I hide myself, they will come and kill you all. So, it is better for me to die".

The killers came with three cars led by the leader of the district. Someone pointed to the exact place where my husband was hiding, which was next door to my late best friend, Mukambuzi's house.

It was horrible. He said to her, "Let me show myself to them". He sacrificed his life for others. The killers took him in their cars and shot him just around 500 meters from our house. The inhabitants testified his body stayed at the roadside for three days, and then two unknown volunteers dug a hole for his body to rest.

Hero, Late Joseph Nyagatare 1952-1994

The grave on the roadside where he was killed

After his death, the génocidaires returned to raid my house. A good neighbour who had a soldier living with them stood up against them. The soldier confronted them saying, "We know that you just killed him, now leave his house alone as his children will inherit it."

This provoked the génocidaires, and they instantly started arguing and fighting among themselves. During the altercation, the soldier shot the man who had killed my husband, right in front of my house. After this altercation, news spread of what had happened.

Tutsis in the area now fled, as they had all became instant targets for the génocidaires. My late husband was known as a very good man, and was genuinely loved everyone. He loved to inspire his students to study and be well-educated to have a glorious future. Till today, there is always a remembrance of the late Nyagatare at the school where he led as the headteacher.

Days went by, and news spread that many of the camp's soldiers were coming with heavy machine guns to kill all the Tutsi inhabitants living at Nyabisindu/Muhanga.

Yet, God proved himself because he is a good God. Most of the Tutsi people fled, hid in the bushes, and the surrounding neighbourhood. The death of my late husband served as a way to protect and save many other people.

Our house and belongings were immediately demolished, and our car was burnt.

My Sorrowful Place

I got informed about the death of my beloved husband, but I could not cry. So, I went to see the religious brothers at their home because they all knew him. I got there and sat down, overwhelmed as I had no one to talk to.

I decided to hide my grief, and I allowed not one single tear to fall. Instead, I had to look for a way to look like a different person. I could not talk to anybody; I was speechless.

The news began to spread all over in the city, and people started to make strong and baseless accusations against me, saying that I was the one who shot the soldier. The owner of my workplace began to spread messages in the city that I should also be killed. I was disturbed and anguished, and sorrow took hold of me like a woman in labour. I got the wisdom to cover up my face and disguise myself.

I put dark ashes on my face and neck, and shaved my hair. I exchanged my clothes with a wonderful young woman who was very kind, caring and compassionate.

There is power in the tongue; the power of good words fought for me.

My words were: "My God, do not let anyone touch me so that, I will be able to take care of my children."

Do not give up on your dreams, as long as they are in line with the Will of God. We shall not dwell on the storm, but we should allow only Jesus Christ to be in our boat. The boat symbolises out body, and our hiding place in God.

Starving for 40 Days

Many Tutsis, including myself, were hiding at Saint Joseph High School College. As a way to make us suffer, the tap water supply and electricity were cut off from our hiding place. Other premises of Kabgayi, like the hospital, doctors' house, the Bishops and Priest's dwellings, had everything including food and water, while we were left to suffer in starvation and dehydration.

As time passed, I saw many old people lying down on the plain ground —dying of thirst and hunger. I held a two-litre water plastic container with water and I remember sharing it with them, giving a lid of water or two to everyone. I was moved with compassion regardless of the circumstance, and I silently said in my heart, "Let me do good in sharing this bottle of water with the dying ones", as I did not want to die with sin.

Where did I get water from? A woman found me and paid back the three thousand FRW she owed me. At that time, it was a significant amount of money, but it is now the equivalent of three pounds. The lady had told me then, as she was handing the money to me, "I don't want to die with your debt".

I was grateful, and I used the money to pay 100 FRWS Rwanda (equivalent to 10 pence in the UK) to the people who were not afraid of dying anymore, to get outside to the river for water.

I lived forty days without eating food, I occasionally drank water from time to time when I could find a volunteer to search for water from the river far for us- though some were killed on the way without returning to my hiding place.

We should always remember to pay back our debts. I received a huge blessing from her returning the money she owed me. The lady is also a survivor.

Entrance of Génocidaires at St Joseph Kabagayi

Daily Slaughter

Each day, groups of Génocidaire (Interahamwe) would arrive to take refugees and they would slaughter them around the bush trees of Kabgayi, until flies and a foul odour of dead bodies took over the place.

There were no tears, arguments, complaints, grief or any retaliation against killers, and everyone was just waiting for their turn and wishing to be killed with guns, rather than with machetes and swords.

One day, I was walking to the only public toilet around when the génocidaires came in. I recognised one of the guys holding a gun- He was the man who used to inform us about all the plots, and about the list of people the Génocidaires planned to kill.

I slightly bent down and sat down on the ground, which was very dirty due to the fermented urine, faeces, and water. I got a revelation to bow down, and hide my face to protect myself. I told myself this man with the gun was no longer a friend and he would probably kill me.

Truth is, friends and neighbours who know you, would most likely be one of the first people to plot against you or kill you. Many people were taken, and slaughtered just around Kabgayi in the bush; some of which were my colleagues and friends.

Some of my friends I would like to remember include; the late Frere Fidele (Headteacher of College Saint Joseph, Gervais teacher of ACEJ College), Louis and his wife Mercy Munyeshuri, Gashagaza, Mutihimura and Children, Mukenke, Kayumba, Gatera and Wife, Nzaramba Malachiya and His wife and niece, Papias, and Muganga.

During all these horrible days, God was with me because I had an extraordinary destiny. I never ceased to talk with God during that dreadful period. I would say:

"Oh Lord, I am not among the dead. I will live and take care of my children. Oh God, do not let anyone touch me. For the sake of the extreme suffering of Christ Jesus, have Mercy on us and all nations of the world."

I believe the confession of our mouth has adequate power, because God said he created us to have dominion.

On the 8th day of May in 1994, the soldiers and Interahamwe (Génocidaires) came to my side early in the morning. I was lying on the floor, and one soldier spotted and recognised me. While pointing at me, he forced me to get out with arrogance and terror.

"Forgive and have mercy on me, my brother, for God is watching you." I begged him. He asked me for money, and I told him that I only had two thousand FRW. After I spoke, he left and said, "I am going, but others will not leave you".

That very day many Tutsi people were killed.

To this day, I can't remember the face of the soldier because of the trauma I suffered from that incident.

On another day, one of the Marist Religious Brothers who was a supervisor, warned me he had been informed the génocidaires planned that night to come to finish me. I begged him to find another hiding place for me. He took me into another classroom where refugees were hidden, and I proceeded to lay on the floor all night. I soon discovered that on my left side, there were dead bodies behind me.

To God be the glory, I survived that night. I love the word of my mouth, specifically God's word.

I moved to another hiding place — this was "The Chapel" of the school. This was a shelter, a refuge, and a shield in the house of God. The refugee that also doubled as the supervisor in charge, warned me the only place remaining for me to hide was the priest's altar, but alas the priest had said not to allow anybody to sit there.

The compassionate supervisor advised me to sneak up to the altar late at night to lie down. He also warned me to leave the altar area early in the morning to avoid being seen. Throughout this period, day after day, the killers kept coming and taking people, but God's grace was upon me.

The Truth fought for me. God had a good plan, and my destiny was not yet accomplished. He has the final word. If God is for you, who can be against you? No man can stop you. Nobody! The angels of God encamp around those who fear Him and deliver them out of trouble.

I continually covered myself up with black ashes, and my hair was constantly shaved. This served as my disguise, as I thought it would help me avoid being discovered easily.
I exchanged clothes with another lady to further help my

disguise gimmick. My borrowed garments empowered me, and I was confident I would not die because I couldn't be recognized. The only thing I wore under the borrowed garment was my late husband's short pants, while holding on to my university degree and his photo in my pocket.

I kept mute most of the time, to the extent that people nearly thought I was mad. I prayed constantly; in the morning, at twelve noon, at three, and at four. I always kept on praying and silently muttering the same words over and over to God "I will not die, but I will live and look after my children."

The Truth that fights daily was based on The Lord's prayer. "Our father in Heaven, hallowed be your name, your kingdom come. Your will be done on earth as it is in heaven. Give us today our daily bread. Forgive our sins as we forgive those who sin against us and lead not into temptation but deliver us from the evil one'.

Though I was petrified, I pretended to be mad and undressed my left breast daily. I would cover myself with black ashes, and bend my head to avoid eye contact with people. Each day was a nightmare, but I learnt to survive.

At the end of May, I recognised one génocidaire with grenades around his waist and panicked, but I confidently hid my fears. I approached him kindly, asking him to tell his mum, who used to be my midwife, to hide me. This guy turned back and promised to do it.

The game was a way to obstruct him from taking people, and I pretended to be friendly with him. The Lord blinded him and I was delivered.

On the last Sunday of May in 1994, the Interahamwe (Génocidaires) came and took many people again, including the lady with whom I had exchanged clothes with. They were all loaded in buses while being in their birthday suits, and were taken to be killed.

The killers came into the chapel and took so many people, but I was left sitting on the floor, bowing down, with my head covered with ashes. They looked at me and said, "Hahaha, this one is finished already".

The camouflage was simply a God-given idea. I am here to tell everyone to stand in faith, and speak over their life with good words. The Truth will stand, and fight a good fight for your good.

Chapter 5
God's Sent Messengers

An army from Heaven came to fight for us and rescued us in a miraculous way to shame the enemies.

With my sister's son, Peter Nyagatere, a Survivor of the genocide against Tutsi

Chapel at St. Joseph School Kabgayi

1st image: My Miracle Day from the grave to life. The entrance of the chapel where I recognised the Inkotanyi, also known as the Rwandan Patriotic Front (RPF), coming to rescue us.

2nd image: My last divine hiding place that I could find during the holocaust. I'm sitting down in the exact spot of the chapel pathway which was the only space I could find amongst other refugees. One of the religious brothers named Christian, removed all the chairs, so we could have enough dwellingroom. When the RPF arrived, this chapel was almost empty as many were killed.

Inkotanyi, the Messengers of Peace as God's Sent

We were all frightened to death after hearing bomb explosions, and shootings around the city.

Suddenly in the morning, we saw on the Fatuma Hill of Kabgayi, a massive number of killers heading towards us, screaming, shouting, and holding all their weapon tools which comprised of mainly machetes, and guns. We watched them speechlessly and full of panic, because we had no means of protecting ourselves or fighting back. We just remained glued to the ground, standing and waiting to die.

I ran back into the Chapel, sat down on the corner at God's "Forbidden Altar" & started to prepare myself to be with God.

My Godly Altar, my hiding place: The image above is the altar where I could go to lay down only in the night, when everyone was asleep. It was my comfort place.

I had my nephew, Peter Nyagatare, with me. I trained him to memorise his name and what he will say to the killers. I further convinced him he was not going to die, and taught him to deny ever knowing me. I also instructed him to tell them he wasn't a Rwandan Citizen, and to memorise his biological mum's name. "If the killer points the finger at you, intensively deny being Rwandan, and tell them you are Congolese". I told him. "Do not be afraid", I reassured Him, "You will live and be united with your biological mum".

After giving all the instructions to my little boy, a woman stood at the door. She shouted and danced joyfully, saying the Inkotanyi had arrived here. Hearing this, I took my little children to the door entrance; and saw the news was true. God's Sent disarmed the enemies.

I identified two people: a survivor friend, Nsabimpuhwe, and the late Ahidu, in company with the RPF soldiers. We were rescued and after seeing these two people, who I couldn't believe were still alive also, my strength was reinvigorated with a strong conviction I was rescued and delivered from death.

On June 2nd, 1994 at Kabgayi, I was called from the grave to life, and I have never forgotten how God sent the messengers of peace to rescue us. I had been tortured physically, been through turmoil; both emotionally and mentally, to the point where I could not talk or cry.

What amazing grace! A miraculous day for many who escaped the atrocity.

We didn't understand how they reached out to us; it was unbelievable. I was shaking, but simultaneously revigorated by seeing them. The Truth will always fight for innocent people.

Fight a good fight, and God will back you up for a significant destiny.

I revealed myself clearly now that the Inkotanyi had occupied the city, and had now arrived to save us. Inkotanyi refers to RPF soldiers, as they named after the militia serving under King Rwabugiri, who was famous for his military conquests, especially in the North of Rwanda. Inkotanyi are referred to as the warrior fighters, that rescued everyone in Rwanda from what could only be described as a satanic plan.

I ran straight to the Inkotanyi, not looking back as my mind said, "This is precious time to either live or to die; save yourself and evacuate the slaughtered place".

Two Inkotanyi men directed me to the safety path and the way out. I continued to walk fast, not looking back though I was exhausted. Then, I saw behind others many people heading in the same direction that was under the control of the RPF.

We followed the warning which was not to walk into the periphery in order to avoid falling into the bomb explosion trap set by the génocidaires. I tied the arm of my little boy Peter with a cord, and attached it to my waist belt, so I could not lose him.

We rested on the open playground, with no covers or blankets for many days and nights. I was very exhausted. I had lost the sense of taste, and smell, and any happiness.

My first sleep was so peaceful.

I continually wetted myself with urine for a week because of the trauma, and because I had no clothes to change into or a place to wash. I wore the same singular pair of clothes from April 23, 1994 to August, 1994. I lived for months, several days, and nights without any form of hygiene.

Today we can become unsatisfied with what we have and take it for granted. Be grateful to God, be thankful wherever you are, and be content.

In the last hours of tribulation and persecution, where hope is almost gone, is when you begin to see miracles happening. God certainly surprised us with His never-ending mercy and loving-kindness.

I am always grateful to the Rwandan Front Patriotic Army of Rwanda; The hands of God were upon them with extreme power and strength to deliver all Rwandan victims.

I surrendered my life and was grateful to God for using such people to fight the good fight. The will of the devil was banished over my life and other soul survivors. I thought it was finished, but I kept my prayers and God delivered me.

God Almighty bless these heroes who rescued us. I am saved to tell others the work of God in what can be described as a horrific lived nightmare.

My song today is that I was raised from grave to life, and I have been taken from grace to grace.

Isaiah 12:1 says, "In that day you will say: O Lord, I will praise; though you were angry with me, your anger is turned away and You comfort me. Behold, God is my Salvation. I will trust and not be afraid; for Yahweh, the Lord is my strength and song; He also has become my salvation."

I recall all the episodes I went through; hiding in bushes, in strangers' houses, and moving to different places for refuge. Women were raped and slaughtered with machetes; thrown alive in the community pit with dead bodies, and some were sexually mutilated. I was rescued alive, not wounded with machetes or knives. I had angels lifting me up all the time.

I met a lady who survived, she had been raped by so many Rwandan génocidaire men in 1994. As she was about to die, they left her in agony. The Truth fought, and she survived the brutality of the rape. She was not to die, but to live to testify the goodness of God.

My late best friend died after a génocidaire tortured her by raping her. The génocidaire then used a sharpened wooden stick to pierce her from her private part to her head.

We are to honour the survivors, and not forget the heroes of the Rwandan Patriotic Front for what they went through. We are also to glorify God, who has a good plan for all human creation.

I am grateful to the Rwandan Patriotic Front, and the Army Forces; who fought a good fight to save humanity. Many lost their lives here on earth; and I truly hope they receive a reward in Heaven. God led them to reach out to us at Kabgayi within the premises of Saint Joseph school college, where we lived in the pit of hell.

The fruits of the great sacrifices by the Forces Army 'Inkotanyi' are that all Rwandan people are now free from discrimination. We have the freedom to live, and never again be called cockroaches. God trained and empowered them to fight the good fight for all the people. I was rescued and saved from premature death, so I can testify.

Today in Rwanda, there is zero tolerance of any denomination of either Hutu, Tutsi or Twa; likewise for zero tolerance for division.

We are all the same humans created by God; the division has been wiped out, and banned forever. Rwanda is a nation currently promoting love, peace, unity, and prosperity to everyone.

For this reason, my heart sings daily again. According to Isaiah 12:4, "And in that day, you will say, praise the Lord call upon his name; declare His deeds among the people, make mention that His name be exalted. Sing to the Lord, for He has done excellent things, this is known in all the earth."

There will be challenges surrounding you, because you are somebody with a great destiny. Check your circumstances, and you will discover your way out and how to reach your goals, vision, and your dreams. Never give up upon God, and upon the

Lord Jesus Christ. God is good, and His Mercy endures forever and ever.

My miracles manifested in my faith and by speaking to God my Father. I questioned myself: "Why have I survived the daily killing that spanned 40 days at Kabgayi?"

My response is "to tell nations and generations and prepare them for the second coming of Christ."

Just stand firm, for the Spirit of excellence is with you. My tongue saved me, the Truth fought for me. The army was sent out speedily to deliver the remaining, and I am grateful for the Rwandan Patriotic Front (RPF). Some died on the way, running to rescue us, while risking their lives for others. The ones who remained fought till the end and saved many innocent Rwandan citizens.

After hiding at St. Joseph College for 40 days with no food, I lost my sense of taste for food. I survived on only water, which was very scarce to find. I had bites all over my body from lices. We had no form of security while other premises of Kabgayi had soldiers around the gates. I appreciate all the men; who spent all their nights outside the classrooms to allow women and children get a place to lie down.

During these times of torture, we never cried, or grumbled or quarrelled, we just waited and kept anticipating to die. Not even the babies or children cried or whined, fear was utterly palpable.

June 2nd, 1994 was a day I had longed and dreamed of; a day of freedom, and a day my hope was realised. After fifty-five days and nights in an unimaginable nightmare, God heard my heart and sent forth calvary to rescue us. What shall I say unto the Lord? What do I have to say but thank you, Lord. There is power in the word of your mouth.

God answered my prayer to live, and to take care of my children. Even though, I knew their father was now in Heaven, it was my time to take up my mantle to care for them sincerely.

My dearest reader, be comforted in whatever you ask God, because it will be granted to you. Believe he will never leave you, nor forsake you. Reject any negative thinking over your life, and focus on the future.

The lyrics by the talented Stormzy from the song titled "Blinded by your grace" beautifully articulates the journey of my heart, and often a remembrance of my resuscitation.

The Truth fought for us, and brought the genocide to an end once and for all. From the despair; hope grew, and God saved the population of Tutsi and the entire Rwandan Nation against this holocaust.

You shall never stand against the nation of God, for He created man in His own image. Whoever is against the innocent shall never succeed over the truth. We must always keep our peace, and let the Lord God fight for us.

Chapter 6
My Stormy Experience

"You can be in the storm, but don't let the storm get in you" – A proverb.

A.   My Baby Died in my Feeble Hands

On my journey to a more secure location led by the soldiers, my two-year-old son, David Ricardo Nyagatare, died in my feeble hands. I was devastated, and I allowed the pain, and sorrow engulf me. The cause of his death was due to our living conditions; he was exhausted from hiding with me in bushes, being bitten by insects and mosquitoes, and the continuous starving at Kabgayi.

We couldn't linger in that location for much longer, so I wrapped his body into my only wrap cloth I had on me. I found two men to help dig a tomb; they were also hopeless but they offered their help regardless.

All hope was gone, but I mustered the courage to be strong and I continued the journey.

A Picture of my Late Son David Ricardo Nyagatare

Devasted to see my boy lifeless, I hated everyone. I went mute, and shed no tears with no fear. My only hope was to run away to another safe pasture.

B.   Stepping Hill from Despair

A staff member of a Non-Government Agency (N.G.O) came to us in search of a translator. I was the only survivor left to translate the French language into Kinyarwanda.

I asked if she could take me to another reliable, and safer location known as Nyamata. To my amazement, she agreed and I instantly knew it was God intervening in my predicament. He had sent this person to help me.

I relocated with a family friend and another survivor, whom I met on my way. This new location was an open field, with striking visible elements of nature. I could see God was working and making a way for me. Once again, he had sent a divine helper to my rescue.

During my time at this new location, a government local authority personnel of the Rwandan Patriotic Front came and recognised me, but I couldn't remember who he was. He left, and then after a few minutes, he sent someone with the uttermost humility and respect to offer me shelter. He accepted I could come with my friend, and the accompanying survivor. He finally introduced himself as my late husband's ex-student in Burundi.

The trauma of what I had been through had wrecked my memory; I could not remember him at the time. I prayed for him, and asked God to bless him because of the kindness he showered upon us. This kind man took me along with people, who had been with me during this journey.

No matter what you do, always do your job well, for the rewards await you when you least expect them. This compassion that was being shown towards me was a reward from the integrity of my late husband's good deeds.

He offered me a beautiful bedroom with beddings and a blanket, and my friends were given another bedroom. I was speechless. I was filthy, and right there I had my first wash after I had spent four months covered with ants and lice.

You can't imagine how I was even scared to use the beautiful beddings offered. From that moment on, my life changed, and I recovered my hope to live and see my children again.

I love God and I have to tell you to love the God of Heaven too; Love Jesus and surrender your life to Him. There are many trials along our journey against us to fulfil our purpose, but you will overcome all, for victory belongs to Him.

My tools for battle were being committed to prayer, speaking forgiveness over my sins and acknowledging God's power to save us, and defeat the génocidaires.

I continually declared the word to live, and not to die. God Almighty honoured his word!

Another staff of the NGO needed a translator, so I was appointed to translate French to Kinyarwanda again between the charity team and the surviving population.

C.   Post Liberation Rwanda Genocide (4 July 1994)

July 4th, 1994 was an unforgettable day, extremely beautiful and enjoyable. The Rwandan Patriotic Front "Inkotanyi" rescued all the Tutsi population from the torment of death, and liberated us to live freely; thereby enabling us to acquire the right to live again.

After this episode, I commenced the search for my late husband's grave. I managed to return to my home, but the challenges before me were so heavy. I returned broken hearted to find all my houses demolished. The killers and génocidaires had even burned our car. The surviving population were surprised of my return and they kept asking "How did I survive?".

I was surprised that even though our car was burnt, the engine remained unburnt and functional. It was miracle! A neighbour assisted in refurbishing the burnt vehicle's remains. I went to claim my car, and the mechanic gave it back to me without any complications; I recall him telling me. "The enemy dug a hole for you, but God made away out for you".

I was very frustrated, and lived in emotional pain and bitterness daily against the perpetrators of the genocide, even against their relatives. I decided to be strong and courageous. I did my best to look after my orphans, and other orphans of unknown parents who were without shelter or support.

Grave of my Late Husband Discovered

The neighbours roughly located the area where he was buried, but no one would show me the exact tomb. I went to the place, and began looking for any signs of bullet remnants that may lead me to him.

An unknown woman who watched me through her compound, came to me. I could tell she was scared to approach me, but she still came over to where I was and showed me the grave.

I was more than relieved. My brother and two old friends secretly dug the grave out to identify him, and they confirmed it was my beloved Joseph. He was still wearing his commonly known coat.

My brother knew that with all the trauma I had experienced, I would not have the heart to look at his body, so he identified Joseph on my behalf.

The neighbour gave a statement of his death, and told us those who were responsible for his death. Many people came to testify about his death.

I was greatly troubled from within, equally restless; but I managed to hide my sorrow, sadness, and fear.

D.   The Devastating Search of my Family-in-law in Butare

I went to Ruhashya, Butare in Rwanda on a two-hour drive to see if I could find any survivors from my in-law's side of the family. It was a disconcerting moment, as I was met with several demolished houses of my in-law's family. My in-law's family members were either slaughtered, or stabbed, or mutilated with machetes and swords. A grand total number of forty-two people were killed in my in-law's family.

My father in-law, Didas Kabayiza, who had lost his hearing and sight, was also a victim of the genocide. I found this demonstration of inconceivable hate troubling because how can a man that couldn't see or hear still be targeted.

I would like to take this opportunity to honour the lives of the individuals from the Kabayiza lineage, they are gone but never forgotten;

- Karambizi Fidele and his wife, Mukagahima Cecile, with their children: Mukagashugi Mediatrice, Mukantaganda Anesia, Benemaliya Bernadette, Mugabe Protogene, and Niyomugabo Emmanuel.

- Athanase Gakwaya and his wife, Mukangamije Rangwida, with their children: Gashagaza Juvens, Gatarayiha Anselme, Rutayisire Eutaria, Mukansoro Beata, Rutayisire Modeste, and Kayitare Eric.

- Mukashyaka Thereza, her children, Uwase Iluminata, Nkusi Emile, Christine, Vestine, and Diogene.
- Melanie with her, children; Kigenza Eugene, and Uwizeye Gonzalv.

- Twagirumukiza Vianey with his wife, Mukankunsi Console and their children: Ephfraim, Prospere, Twagirayezu Jean Damacene, Uwaringiyimana Vestine, Athanasia, Valentine, Marie Grace, Shema Claude, and Claudine.

- Niyonsenga Gisele, Uwamariya Solange, and Mutesi Sandra

I would also like to remember the lives of my aunties, uncles and their wonderful families who were victims of the genocide;

- Filomena Mukangamije, with her four children who were thrown to their death in the toilet sewage.

- Pacal Sekaganda; and his, wives, eight children, thirteen grandchildren, two daughter in-laws, and son in-law.

- The family of Uncle Selestini; his ten children and two wives.

Fortunately for me, I found two little girl that survived the genocide. I ended up taking care of them and raising them. They were traumatised, and the month of April brought back horrid memories each year for them, as it was the worst time of their lives. One of them was present when the génocidaires killed her family. She ran to her neighbour for hiding, and this family helped her to hide. Eventually, she was later made to remain in their field rearing goats. She was just ten years old when all this transpired.

The land was vast, but I chose to abandon my search, for it was not safe to stay or even to explore further. For my sake and safety, I abandoned the land and never returned to search for answers, or to find the killers to obtain some form of justice for my beloved family.

Who Really Hears Our Cries?

Some time had passed, before I went in search for the grave of my late son, David. I located the area, but I couldn't see the grave, sadness gripped me because I desired to reunite with my boy.

People came to help me search, but they could not find the grave. My friends and I decided to leave and go home. Before leaving I sat down in the field, soaked in tears. I told God then: "You have opened my womb and given me this boy. You took Him, and now you don't want to show me his grave, so I am going back home."

God surely heard my cry, because suddenly I saw a blooming sunflower; which reminded me of the flowers I had left on the tomb. I ran to it, and I screamed questionably, "This is the place?" Finally, the grave of my sweet innocent David was found. I took his body home for the burial, and finally put him in a resting place next to his father. I was glad he was not alone anymore.

This encounter has continually reminded me to always open my heart to God. We should not be discouraged by people or circumstances. God hears our cries, whispers, and in return directs us in the right path. Trust Him; God is the same yesterday, today, and forever.

Call upon God, be bold and speak to your father in Heaven. Faith in Him displaces all obstacles. Faith is the key leading to a glorious day. He says "Ask it shall be given unto you; knock the door, and it shall be opened; seek, you will find". Faith enabled made me to cross the red sea of challenges and dwell in the land of the living.

Trials and tribulations prepare us to enter the great destiny that God has planned for us.

E. Rain After the Storm

All my families that were refugees since 1959 in the Republic Democratic of Congo, joined me and brought back some of my older children who escaped the killing in 1994.

I cared for us all, providing for the needs of everyone without complaining or arguing.

The grace and mercy of God made me so strong, and till date, I strive to be a positive and fruitful person.

I started to build my life again from scratch. The challenges were intense; as I was a widow full of bitterness anger, and I was mentally traumatised.

I am thankful to God for putting the minister, late Aloyisia Inyumba, and the excellent staff, Mr Karega Vincent, in my path through another divine helper, Johnson Mugaga.

The honourable late minister, Aloysie Inyumba, fought a good fight to restore communities. She poured value back into women and families. The widows, single parents, and orphans that were separated from their relatives could now build their life back with confidence again.

Through this lifting up, I managed to remain positive. I too had a heart of compassion to support, and strengthen everyone to come out of poverty; especially women and orphans.

During this significant turning point of the country, societal norms had also started to shift. Historically, the culture and tradition had minimized the potential gifts and talents of women.

Thus, publicly ignoring their role in the country's development. A new Rwanda was emerging, as the government promoted women, widows and single mothers, and married women to be valued in all activities to rebuild the country.

I was part of the women leading this initiative, and I worked with an organisation that was devoted to helping and supporting women; and families through the trauma of the genocide. We were able to achieve many things; like facilitating the building of homes of widows, and searching for donors to help build a women's centre in Muhanga district.

Though I loved my career, I was miserable because of the devastating killings of the entire lineage of my in-laws, my husband, and my son. I would sadly reflect on my early widowhood, and how I was left to cater for my children without their father present.

I hated everyone, and I was always singing sorrowful songs anytime I remembered 1994 genocide incident. I had two maid servants and a security guard, but I still couldn't sleep at night; as I feared the killers would return to eliminate us at any time.

I was aware the génocidaires that were hidden could deceptively use the maidservants to poison us through the food we eat. At dinner time, I would always force everyone to share food on the same tray, to avoid any food poisoning ordeal that might have been prepared by the maidservant.

At that time, the hidden killers could break through the windows and throw grenades inside the house. I placed a heavy wardrobe on my bedroom window to protect us and keep my sanity intact. The fear and trauma were too much, but I was still courageous notwithstanding. I majorly focused on the education of all my children, and the orphans I cared for. I would regularly put on a fake smile publicly, and pretend to be joyful but I was miserable on the inside.

Frequently, I visited the graves of my loved ones that were dead with flowers every weekend, ensuring the place was cleaned. I occasionally organised mass services for prayers of their remembrance. Years after years, dwelling on the past affected my sleeping patterns.

F. Looking Up

I developed psychological trauma and hatred. I lost all hope, but I kept fighting to be a good mother.

I worked in a community village and on a particular day, a teenage girl who was also a survivor asked me, "Please can you take me to your home?" Moved with compassion and mercy, I accepted to take care of her. The girl had lost all her relatives and families in the genocide in the 1994 Rwanda. She had also been mutilated with machetes, and then thrown alive in a pit filled with dead people.

Though I was still battling with trauma, I felt compassion toward young women and children who were survivors' of 1994 genocide. I loved helping groups of women trying to find solutions to various troubling issues; alongside other excellent team workers. The likes of Mr Kanture Damian, and Mrs Mukaremera Godelaine, also assisted in finding solutions to the women's problems.

One particular example of the work we did was supporting an eleven-year boy that had finished primary school, and had no parents to further his education. We suggested contacting authorities to find help for this young boy, and they gave him all he needed to continue with his studies.

He was a very clever boy and needed a good school, and with the support of the government, we were able to do just that. One early morning, this same boy came knocking on my gate, and I went to meet him. He said, "I am an orphan, and the only surviving person of my family, but my uncle has refused to keep me in his house".

My first thought was to send the boy back, but a word came into my heart: "Oh, this is a child of God sent to you. You better take him in". I thought to myself, this could be the Lord Jesus who came in the form of a boy.

I accepted the boy to be raised in my family. He was smelling, and he had no clothes. Apparently, my older son and the young boy were of the same age. My older son accepted him instantly, and gave him beautiful new trousers and shirts.

I said to my son, "No. Do not give him the new ones, give him the old ones. I just bought these ones for you." My son answered me by saying "Mum, he deserves good ones, not the old ones". I nurtured this boy for years, and to the glory of God, the orphan boy became a medical doctor.

My son taught me never to give anybody unwanted clothes. Till today, I make sure I donate valuable things to people in need. My home became a resting place for the people in need, and also for orphans.

God opened the door to many other children who were in need of care. Another survivor brought an orphan girl survivor; who was tied to a tree during the genocide, and then left alive. The girl has now grown to become a wonderful woman, and mother to many children.

After surviving, I felt the need to be available to help people in need. Though I was traumatised, I was ever grateful for the goodness, mercy, and faithfulness of God for saving me from premature death.

Working in the community was a good opportunity to help women get restored emotional, and psychological. The majority were widows; and single mothers without their own houses. The grace of God led our team, alongside government support and non-government organisations. We built houses and trained numerous women.

I met a widow who had been rejected by her family-in-laws and they had taken over her land and possessions. She was made homeless because she had no child of her own. I went to her community; some witnesses testified of her right to the land, and the belongings.

I didn't have a stamp, but we wrote down the witness statements. Some people had not been to school, so everyone put their fingerprints as their signature pledge for the lady to be given all her possessions back.

The lady took the report statement to the highest level of government authority, and got back her rights to everything that had been forcefully taken from her. I was grateful, and the lady gave me a nickname, which can be translated to "The woman who doesn't have a stomach ache". I was truly elated that she was restored.

When God is for you, who can be against you?

I lived with the psychological hurt from the tragic happenings of the genocide and its side effects, still I never ignored helping others.

G. Storm of Explosion due to Ambush

Time to time, I lived with fear daily and was very traumatised as some of my friends that had survived were killed by hidden génocidaires. Many other survivors were stabbed to death as they were seen as survivor witnesses. Thus, they could give factual statements about other people that were killed.

On an early Sunday morning, I decided to go to the church. As I was about to get up and prepare to leave, my youngest daughter who sharing the bed with me refused to put on the light. She said "Mummy, do not switch on the light. Put off the light while we are sleeping."

I listened to her, and decided to remain in bed with lights turned off. A few minutes after, a neighbour came walking down from the pedestrian pathway into our compound to greet my maidservant, as he was always friendly with them and was once my catering staff.

At the entrance gate, he found a grenade set as an ambush. The young man came to wake me up, and told me about the horrible trap at the main entrance gate's house. I jumped up quickly to escape with my little child.

Psalms 23 says, "The lord is my shepherd; I shall not want.........
He prepares a table before me in the presence of my enemy"

Once again, I saw again the Hand of God shielding me.

I took my daughter, and we began to escape. A neighbour urgently called the attention of the soldiers to where the grenade was placed. They immediately came to remove it from our habitation and I saw a massive smoke. I witnessed a very horrible explosion.

This situation was clearly a sign for me as I was targeted to be killed by the génocidaires that were still hidden in the midst of the populace. The period was perilous as I knew some of my surviving friends were killed in the same city; so there would be nobody to testify about the horrific events perpetrated by the génocidaires.

I became more restless, worrisome, and fearful. I had a close friend who cared for my wellbeing deeply. Every moment she heard any shooting of guns or explosions, she would rush to check if I was still alive.

There was a day I went around greeting my neighbour across the road; as soon as she saw me, she broke into tears. I asked her why she was crying and she answered, "Can't you flee? The hidden Interahamwe will kill you. See the grenade ambush that you just escaped."

I told her that I was not going to be a refugee again, and reassured her not to worry. I pretended to be fine, but my heart was burning with fire, but I could only smile to hide the fear in my heart. I believe God sent this woman to warn me divinely. My eyes were opened after, I knew I needed to be realistic and find a safe place to hide.

It is very important to be nice to our neighbours wherever we find ourselves. Some of them are like good Samaritans who truly care with compassion.

If God is for you, who can be against you? He is our refuge, our shield, our helper, our fortress, and our rock. He will never leave us nor forsake us. His angels encamp around those who fear Him to protect us and deliver us out of our troubles.

We are created for God's glory and to shine. Put your trust in the Lord. Psalm 115:11 says, "You who fear the Lord, trust in the Lord; He is their help and their shield."

Psalm 116: 8-9 also says, "For you have delivered my soul from death, my eyes from tears and my feet from failing. I will walk before the Lord in the land of the living".

God continually wants us to strengthen others, knowing that though the tears may last for the night, but joy comes in the morning.

Chapter 7
Voodoo, Wizards & Attendant Loss.

'The child of an elephant will never be a dwarf' – A Nigerian Proverb.

Disasters, challenges, or success - are the results of what we say through our tongue. They reflect our work in the world. We are tested to fulfil our destiny each glorious day. To enjoy a joyful life, there is a price to pay.

Success requires hard work, and utmost trust in the Maker of Heaven to achieve the given goals. We all have the potential to have dominion on Earth as God revealed in his word. However, the practices we embrace through our ungodly cultures, and traditions cause many to lose out in the destiny race, thereby, missing God's purposes and plan.

A.   Following the Ungodly

Trials, failures, and pressures of life push people to search for answers. In listening to different opinions, including from our cultural and ancestral backgrounds, many generations are seduced and introduced to the kingdom of darkness. These places might appear to have relevant solutions to the problems, but might end up getting us deeper and deeper into traps we may later regret in life. Following all this advice, and opinions are sometimes the cause of human woes.

My mum had died earlier, and left eight children to be catered for by my dad. Her premature death raised suspicions that she was killed through witchcraft, by one of the family members. This led my father to search for protection as any protective father would ordinarily do. Eventually, he found another voodoo priest to counter such evil against our family.

The priest later revealed to my dad that his late wife was a victim to envy and jealousy. Therefore, he had to protect his children.

This voodoo man started making incisions on various parts of our bodies. This, he claimed, would ward off any form of witchcraft responsible for our mother's untimely death. I was his first victim.

I was considered the eldest because my older sister was already married. He started using a sharp knife to leave marks of incisions on my body, on my chest, and on my lower belly. He further applied unknown herbs and black powder on the incisions.

I couldn't cry, even though I was in severe pain. It was so bad that my elder brother ran away after watching these manipulations.

He shouted and declared the practice was unacceptable, and the man had to leave as it was a sham. The voodoo man became extremely embarrassed and decided to leave our house. All my other siblings were saved from this incident; and unfortunately, I was the only victim.

The same thing happened to me when I started college at the young age of 15. I was sent to live with a family friend for short period. During my stay with them, they coerced me to have more alterations done to my body, to protect me from untimely death like that of my mother.

She made incisions underneath my breast on both sides, and above my pubic region with a sharp small knife. She covered it up with ashes of herbs. She later stated the reason for this was that she was protecting me from premature death.

I was a young obedient girl, but they abused my innocence and humility. The effect of these wicked acts on my body left me devastated as my life became miserable.

Prior to this, I was brilliant in my academics. Just after the various incisions, my academic performance began to drop to the extent that, I failed my final year examination in college.

Right after the incision incident, we started recording more catastrophes in the form of death in my family. Shockingly, my grandmother also passed away within six months after my mother's death. We didn't have peace at home after the tragic death of my mom. All my siblings grew up with my dad, and I was the only child separated from the family.

In 1993, I owned a small corner shop, selling daily goods such as sugar, rice, beans alcohol, and essential daily items. One day, thieves entered my shop in my absence and emptied the entirety of the shop. I was angry, and I foolishly went again to look for a voodoo man, to help me identify who the robbers were, because I wanted to get them arrested. The voodoo man asked me to pay him a huge amount of money, and I complied.

With the money, he bought a dead sheep and buried it underneath the footprints of the robbers. He told me the people who stole your goods would be arrested. The period coincided with the anniversary of the exact day I became a widow (April,1994). I never saw any good outcome from the voodoo man's prediction, as all he said were just pure lies.

From my experience, I am telling everyone not to trust in voodoo men or wizards because they will waste your money and time. Just believe in God and your life will not be the same. My life became modified only after I surrendered all my worries to God.

I have been rescued to tell everyone, to get out from ungodly thoughts and doctrines. Give your life entirely to Him.

Though I survived the 1994 genocide in Rwanda, at times I

was not thankful to God. I lived in sorrow and bitterness. I was smiling, but suffering from the death of my husband, my son, and my entire in-laws. I was not faithful to God, who brought me out of the grave into life. I started to fight the enemy by myself, and follow the world's system. I never had peace or joy, and sleeping at night became a big problem.

I have now learnt to be thankful and faithful to God. Do good to your friends, and do not fulfil the worldly desires of the flesh. All the tests in my life were preparing me to enter my great destiny.

Never trust any voodoo man or wizard. I was a victim to all these practices and suffered for a long time.

In spite of my failed experiments, it was evident that I had not learnt any lesson from the deceit and the disappointment of previous voodoo men. In 1999, I followed a friend to another voodoo witch in a village. She was known as a 'Good one' in terms of giving revelation, and prophecies of what will happen in an individual's future. She claimed to always protect people by giving them concoction of herbs, roots of plants and ashes.

Unfortunately, I trusted her again, and spent money in buying various goods and articles for the ritual. While practising one of her tricks, she took us into one of her rooms; and consulted terrestrial sources.

The result of this evil consultation affected me, and my life became worse in fear. It took a long time to come out of this voodoo scheme, until I repented of my sins and believed in Jesus Christ as my Saviour. He called me out of the darkness into His marvellous light.

Do not dedicate your life to idols; there are consequences when you put your trust in those practices. Do not waste your time and finances in consultation with any voodoo, witchcraft, and wizard machinery. In the process, you are inadvertently exposed to failures that can gradually ruin your life.

If you have ever been exposed to these types of mystic forces, the only way out is to repent of your sins and believe in Christ Jesus as your Lord and Saviour.

Our life is precious, and we should strive to protect it, and focus on the promises of God.

B. The World and its Failures

"It's failure that gives you the proper perspective on success"
- Ellen DeGeneres

You build on failure by using it as your stepping stone. Don't try to forget the mistakes, but don't dwell on them. You don't let it have any of your energy, or any of your time, or any of your space."
- Johnny Cash

Looking back, I was married in a Catholic church; but I did not bother attending church. I had really backslidden.

After I discovered I was pregnant, I went to consult a voodoo witch. She told me, "Oh woman, the baby will be born without complications, but I can see one of your children will pass away". These declarations were made through the reading of my palms and through my eyes. I was not prayerful then, so I kept quiet instead of rebuking it.

With unceasing prayers and supplications, we need to check out our lives and never bow to idols; trusting God only is the key to being blessed. Do not sit in the counsel of wicked people; depart from such and ask God to direct you to the right person.

I urge everyone, do not harbour evil intentions in your minds or speak terrible words over your lives or your beloved ones. The wrong declaration blocks us from moving into our purposes.

There is a strong power in prayer when your faith, love and hope are consistently centred in Christ, and line with the will of God. When you trust the doers and practices of carnal magic, the consequences will destroy your purposeful life.

I will advise everyone to keep trusting God; whatever you need will appear along the way as long as you've placed your trust in Christ.

The word of says that "Those who are willing and obedient will eat the fruit of the land" (Isaiah 1:18). This means that only those that obey the will of Christ will eat the fruit of the land and be blessed.

My disobedience caused me to lose all that I had. I had an excellent lifestyle; houses, and maidservants, but I lost everything. I was left with nothing, to the point of having no clothes at all, no home or photographs as a memory. All I had with me was my University Degree Certificate folded in the pocket of my trousers.

After the 1994 genocide in Rwanda, I started to build my life again and became a strong woman. Later, I became worried and traumatised as survivors were killed clandestinely, so I decided to find refuge abroad. I left everything and fled away. I lost my job; I was broken, homeless, and all my family were also shattered.

I remembered all my instances of bowing to idols, voodoo men, witch doctors; led my entire life to be miserable. God humbled me to come to his obedience. My life was a mess because of ignorance, and I nearly perished.

The Grace of God is always available to us. You only have to take the decision to seek him with all your heart. Mathew 6:33 says "Seek the kingdom of God and his righteousness other things will be added unto you".

Avoid being led by different voodoo herbalists and wizards. Trust in God Almighty; only then will you be saved, and your life will have real meaning. The challenges of life are preparing you for your great destiny. The Truth fought for me, and I have learned the lesson not to trust in any voodoo herbalist or wizard.

Chapter 8
My Step-in & European Challenges.

A. Medications

Remember, God's power is displayed when it seems all is finished. He will demonstrate His authority over everything we face. This journey was my hardship. I found myself homeless, helpless, and depressed, for I was very traumatised.

What was my medication? I never stopped telling God "Please help me look after the family I left behind" I would constantly use the Lord's Prayer from Matthew 6:9-13 to pray. It went thus;

"Our father in Heaven hallowed be your name. Your Kingdom come Your Will be done on earth as it is in heaven. Give us this day our daily bread and forgive our sins as we forgive those who sins against us and lead not into temptation. But deliver us from the evil one. For Yours is the kingdom and the power and the glory forever. Amen."

The Lord's prayer has always been a scripture I would regularly meditate on in all the circumstances, and challenges I went through.

Going out during the winter season was my worst experience as I kept falling over on the street. I was admitted to a hostel full of men, and a few women. In the night, men would knock on my door, but I would not open it as I feared they could rape me. Frightened, I reported to the reception and was given a room closer to the security guard. I knew the principles of human rights and claimed them in order to be protected.

Stressed out by the new life, I walked to the sea with tears rolling down my cheeks. My heart started beating strongly, and my chest began constricting. That very day, my anxiety and depression nearly pushed me into the sea, as I had no one to express my emotions to. Before I did something I would later regret, I began reciting the Lord's prayer right then, and ran away from the sea as fast as I could.

I was transferred to another hostel with many men refugees, where I spent one night in. The following morning, I protested. I shouted, crying, "Oh God help me." No way could I sleep again in a place where only men stayed at, and I was then given a better shelter.

Remember, always claim your rights, and positioning yourself for the truth will work out the solution for you. Failure and stress can destroy one's personality, and most people end up being depressed when they are stressed.

God watches over us always, especially during our stormy experiences. Our divine helpers; the angels - fight for us, even in battles that we can't see.

I was praying, repeating the same words over and over again, but I was never thinking of repenting from my iniquities and transgressions. I was only bitter and sorrowful in my homeless state, and I kept thinking of my orphaned children in Africa.

It is the Truth that if we ask, it shall be given; seek; you will find; knock on the door, and it will be opened. Our God is merciful, and gracious and heard my cry —eventually I got a place to live.

B. My First Day on the Street

I decided to go for a walk on the day I was released from the homeless hostel. English language was my biggest barrier to communication. I walked into the city to look for public phone boxes, and I miraculously came across a divine helper who today became my second husband, John Kodjovi.

He patiently guided me to know the city. I learnt how I could live in the city, and communicate with my children who were already scattered from their homeland for their safety.

Through him, I was also connected later to my first Rwandan compatriots. They helped me discover how I could get settled, they even trained to drive and taught me a few computing skills. Rwandan people are good in hospitality and care. Though we all suffered from the impact of the genocide, there is still a heart for communal love.

The journey was not easy. I lived on five pounds weekly because I wanted to save the rest of my money to send back to my children in Africa.

I started to remember the prayers I said during the 1994 genocide in Rwanda; when God saved me from rape, mutilation and gunshots. "Oh God, on account of the astonishing suffering of Christ, have mercy on us and on all nations."

These words were always in my prayer, along with the Lord's prayers. I would pray every day; early in the morning, at noon, by three o'clock, and six o'clock in the evening. The three o'clock afternoon prayer was to remember the hour that Jesus Christ died.

After a very long and strenuous period of searching, I found a job working in a warehouse. I couldn't afford winter shoes at the time, and the warehouse was extremely cold that I couldn't talk while working. My toes got injured due to the cold, I didn't give up and continued to do the job. I remember the first week's payment was like God handing over money to me.

I had the desire to do a post-graduate master's degree, but I abandoned my ambitions as the cost of living for my children discouraged me, as I was the sole bread winner. I ultimately decided to focus on my primary job to supply their needs, and encouraged myself that my children would study and obtain degrees in years to come.

D. The Mystery of Menopause and a Child

My body changed, and I gained weight rapidly, even though I was working hard to feed my family and pay bills. I was exhausted. I used public transport, and I recall every time I sat on the bus - I was always falling asleep. Some days, I would be so engrossed in sleep that I would miss my bus stop.

Some time passed and I started seeing other changes in my body, but I couldn't find an explanation to why. One day, as I ran to catch the bus, I suddenly felt like my womb was heavy, and dropping down. I explained to some people, and the response I got was that I was working too hard labouring in storehouses, lifting heavy things, and moving pallets. Still, the explanation I received wasn't adding up.

I started to feel pain in my lower left belly, but my friends would tell me it was hernia. My belly continued to grow strangely, becoming very big and worrying. At a point, I thought it was a form of sickness that was very common in Europe at that time.

I took medicine tablets from someone to reduce the fluid and fat in my belly. I often would rush to the nearest toilet with the greatest urgency to pass urine. I would also fall asleep on the bus, and would be woken up by my nine-year-old who was at my side, when the bus arrived at our bus stop.

I finally went to the medical centre, but the receptionist did not quite understand my worries due to the language barrier between us. Broken and in tears, I removed my top and exposed my belly to them.

Finally, I got consulted by a doctor. He told me almost instantly without blinking "Oh, you are pregnant."

It was a big shock! "How?", I argued it was not true because I was fifty. I was an old woman. I had hit menopause at that time.

I was urgently referred to a hospital, and the test confirmed that I was very much pregnant. The pregnancy was estimated to be between twenty-six to twenty-seven weeks old. The fear became so much that I told them I was ready for an abortion. The doctor said it was impossible to do because the baby had grown up to a certain stage, and I was at risk of death if I tried to abort the baby. I asked for a caesarean at the time to give birth because I was still scared.

When the contractions began, I went to stay in the hospital, though the nurses advised me to stay at home, but I refused to stay at home.

My baby was delivered, but the post-traumatic stress disorder was so heavy that I could not talk of my pain. I remembered being soaked with tears in the presence of health visitors, as I was unable to explain my trauma. Eight weeks after the birth, I got a job and I was leaving my new-born baby to go to work.

God gave me this testimony in order to tell men and women to support each other to stop abortion, and bring up children to cling to the good morals and values of a good society. The child saved from abortion is now a great person; she became the door for countless benedictions to us.

Deuteronomy 28:12 -13, "The Lord will open to you His good treasure, the heavens, to give the rain to your land in its season, and to bless all the work of your hand…, And the Lord will make you the head and not the tail; you shall be above only, not be beneath if you heed the commandment of the Lord your God, which I command you today, and are careful to observe them."

At twelve years old, she became a choir member in the temple of God. She encouraged me to never stop attending Sunday service. I was also active in the choir and loved serving God. God's reward is a treasure that will come to you when you least expect it, and she was one of my rewards.

We will eat the fruit of our labour if we don't give up on hope, faith, and love.

1 Corinthians 13:13 says: "Now abide faith, hope, love, and these three: the greatest is love. For God is love." Speak and focus on miracles coming your way.

Every step and all tests of life prepare us for a better future, for our tomorrow will always be greater than today.

E. Blinded by the First Fake Friend

As a stranger in town, I became friendly to a sixty-year-old woman who seemed noble, caring and full of compassion. This woman told me she was a retired doctor, and I believed her.

Eventually, I discovered she was trying to destroy my second marriage from different angles. When I discovered she was backbiting, I ended the friendship amicably.

Be careful and conscious of the people you volunteer to assist, especially when the person is unfamiliar, and you have no knowledge about their background.

This should serve as a wake-up call to all married, or unmarried couples. The gift of hospitality, with wisdom should be used to protect marriages.

F. Break Down Barriers

The barrier created by my inability to speak English was quite challenging, as I felt I looked foolish whenever I spoke. This resulted in various insults because I could not understand the meaning of what people around me were saying.

The language was my barrier in interacting with others. Gradually, I learnt to communicate, but still lived an isolated life in my neighbourhood. I was just going to work and coming home.

God says In Deuteronomy 31:6, "Be strong and of good courage, do not fear nor be afraid of them; for the Lord your God, He is the One who goes with you. He will not leave nor forsake you."

This verse encouraged me and I kept working hard. I was doing any job to feed my broken and scattered family. I started learning English at my workplace, using the French-English translation dictionary as a guide. I was also using Bibles written in French and English to learn.

This word comforted me throughout the entire escapade. Isaiah 43:2, "When you pass through the waters, I will be with you. Through the rivers, they shall not overflow you. When you pass through the fire, you shall not be burned, no shall the flame scorch you."

Our languages are our primary ways to communicate with one another. Speaking verbally, or non-verbally serves as a source to unite people together.

G. Favoured by Grace

The time came when I decided to search for another job. I approached an adviser in the local job centre. She was so impressed and shocked, when she read my Curriculum Vitae (CV). She asked me why I applied for a cleaning job, I explained to her English wasn't my native tongue.

I was a holder of a University Degree in Chemistry and Biology qualification in teaching. I asked if I could work in the hospital close to me. The following day, she gave me a recommendation letter to take to the recruitment team of the hospital. The words of my tongue had risen once again to pave a better path and future for me.

After they had interviewed all the prospective workers, the coordinator said to the prospective workers present, "If you do not receive a call back by tomorrow, presume you've not been selected". On my way out, I told him, "Honourable, thank you, but I am among the people you will call back. See you again".

Miraculously, the company called me back to commence work in the hospital.

There is power in our affirmations, and when facing obstacles, these assertions have the exceptional energy to break obstructions that lay in the path of our destiny. No doubt, it is good to have counselling in our community to help in times of despair.

My last working place before I retired was at the Salford Royal Foundation Trust in the United Kingdom. I am grateful to have met sister nurses, Helen Unsworthy, and the whole team at the Main Outpatients' Department. They showed kindness and love towards me. Though we were many, I was selected to work in the clinical support section in the outpatient clinics.

I was able to support my family adequately until my retirement. I genuinely loved my job with passion, and I honoured everyone I came in contact with. My dream of working with a good team, and under an excellent leadership system was fulfilled.

From this period of my life onwards, I was integrated into diverse cultures through invitations to various social functions.

July 2015, My First Day Out With Lovely Sisters

Do not lose hope or give up on your dreams; only call upon God. The divine helper is on his way, and angels are fighting for us to be winners, and not the victims. Refuse fear; because we have been given the power to take dominion over every force of fear.

Isaiah 41:10 says, "Fear not for I am with you; be not dismayed, for I am your God. I will strengthen you. Yes, I will help you. I will uphold you with my righteous right hand."

H. Fruits of our Handwork Speaks Volumes

Talking to God frequently showed me He is always watching over everyone, especially in times of trouble, call upon Him, and He will answer.

Years back, I helped families in different ways. I helped an old lady, and she told her children about the work I had done for her. In one of my hopeless times, one of my children stayed with that same woman I helped, and my child was well-loved and protected.

Another family showed this exact same kindness to my daughter. After hearing my story, and of the difficulties life had thrown my way, they asked me: "Could we adopt your child and give you the money?"

This broke my heart, and I rejected the offer. I kept crying to God for mercy. I was fasting, and praying weekly for my family to be reunited.

Never smiling or enjoying life, or even buying clothes, I was content to eat and survive with a simple meal, and by drinking water. After long and intense prayers, the family moved with compassion and mercy took the initiative to send my eight-year-old child to me.

While in the process of joining me, I told my child, "You have no sins. I am a sinner, but you are a saint. Only tell God, "Please have mercy on me and let me go to my mum" That was the prayer of this my child.

Teach your children to speak to God, and you will see the result. Jesus said in Matthew 19:14, "Let the little children come to Me, and do not forbid them; for of such is the kingdom of heaven".

There is power in prayers, and this is why we need to get into the habit of praying. Talking to God has shown me that He is always watching over everyone.

With perseverance, be rest assured you will achieve your dreams. The test will only last for a while, and you will definitely see the hand of God even when all things seem to have failed. I finally saw my miracle, and was able to reunite with my daughter.

Be kind to one another and have a heart of compassion and love. Be a good giver, and avoid being selfish. The sacrifices of the work of your hands will be rewarded at God's time.

Our future is in His hands, and no good work is despised when we are doing the work with all our heart. You will see the fruits of the work of your hand when you least expect it. Learn to plant good seeds by helping others in times of need. The more you support your relatives or friend to achieve a goal, the more you strengthen them for future generations.

Chapter 9
Come to The Fountain of Life

"The fear of the Lord is a fountain of life, to depart from the snares of death."

- Proverbs 14:27 (KJV)

Who do you trust? Who do you fear? Where do you get the provision? Who can revive or restore the broken heart? Is there any fountain that is inexhaustible?

Isaiah 12:3 says, "Therefore, with joy, you will draw water, from the Wells of salvation." The enjoyment of God's bountiful blessings comes through the anointed one, Jesus Christ, who is the source of everlasting life.

A.   Come to the Truth

Buy the truth and do not sell it; the truth is so important we should be willing to pay any price to obtain it. The verse, John 14:6, tells us the Jesus is the way, the truth and the life.

The genocide left scars and trauma over my life, but then again, my vision was not switched off. The Truth that Fights enabled me to pursue my journey, and take care of my orphans. I was restless, sleepless, unhappy, I had multiple nightmares, and was heavy-laden with hatred. The Truth that fought genocide brought my healing; my restoration from all the trauma.

How did it happen?

Isaiah 1:19 says, "If you are willing and obedient, you shall eat the good of the land. But if you refuse and rebel, you shall be devoured by the sword, for the mouth of the Lord has spoken."

Hearing good words can bring transformation, revival, restoration, new visions, and new dreams. There is power in our tongue; it has the ability to kill or the capacity to give life. John 3:16 says, "For God so loved the world that He gave His only begotten Son, that whoever believes in Him should not perish but have eternal life". I heard this word, and it touched my heart.

Romans 6:23 also says, "For we know that the wage of sins is death, but the gift of God is eternal life in Christ Jesus our Lord"

I got to know Pastor Irene and she explained Christianity to me, though I was still narrow-minded, stubborn, and holding on to my past. The pastor formed a group fellowship in my house, which was the start of an in-house Church. Nevertheless, I was not converted, for I was still held hostage by the devil. The evil spirit obstructed me from hearing the Word of the Truth.

I got invited by a friend to the overnight fellowship and prayers. The atmosphere was electric because everyone was jumping, singing, praising, and worshipping the Lord. The Word of God in Romans 10:9 came to me with power saying, "If you confess with your mouth the Lord Jesus and believe in your heart that God raised Him from the dead, you shall be saved"

The guest speaker, Gilbert Sefaranga, threw this question to the audience: "Does anyone want God in their lives"? My past was still haunting me, so I knew I needed God to be in my life. I stepped in front of the congregation, repented and asked God to forgive of all my iniquities and transgressions.

I confessed this prayer "My God, I am a sinner. I repent all my sins. Please forgive me. I believe that Jesus Christ died for me for my sins, so I ask you, Lord Jesus, to come into my heart. I give you, my life."

I have never forgotten the day I gave my life to Christ and became a born-again Christian. Since 2008, I started a long journey to know who God truly is. I loved to go to church for praise and worship sessions. Though I didn't speak good English then, I had the French and English Bibles to find the translations of verses.

I wanted to hear God and see my life change. The scripture in

Revelation 3:20-21 says, "Behold, I stand at the door and knock. If anyone hears My voice and opens the door, I will come to him and dine with him, and he with Me. To him who overcomes I will grant to sit with Me on My throne, as I overcome and sat down with My Father on His throne".

It is never late to come back to God and say, "Lord, I am sorry". He is a faithful, and loving Father who is waiting for us to come back to him. There will be a time when you would need a spiritual, and divine helper to guide you in the way of God.

I am grateful for the life of Prophetess Chi Ezeh, and late Pastor Ephraim Ezeh of Arise and Shine Christian Ministries, who took their time to train me to grow spiritually.

This verse, Joshua 1:8, was my favourite, and I memorised it. It says "This book of the law shall not depart from your mouth, but you shall meditate in it day and night, that you may observe to do according to all that is written in it. For then you will make your way prosperous, and then you will have success".

My ways and thoughts changed, and I took a decision never to look back. I renounced all my evil activities. My friends and relatives tried to discourage me by saying, "Oh, it is only for a short period, wait and see; nothing will work". This was not the case for me. I genuinely stopped trying to justify myself through lies or other bad behaviours. I started my new journey by going to different churches with my family.

One thing didn't leave me though and that was the side effect of the holocaust during the 1994 genocide. My heart was full of bitterness, unforgiveness and hatred. Through the power of prayer, I eventually forgave others. I began to join the prayer night and the Festival of Praise event at Arena in Manchester each year.

My daughter clocked fifteen, and became a choir member in the church. I had to back her up to attend the rehearsal. She was very fervent and faithful in doing good work.
I was always at her side in the winter; both in the good and bad weather seasons. I had a blanket and stayed in the car until the end of each practice.

I never gave up, and this motivated me not to miss any service on Sundays.

There is a scripture that encouraged us - Hebrews 10:24-25. It says, "And let us consider another to stir up love and good works. Not forsaking the assembly, for yourselves together as is the manner of some, but exhorting one another, and so much the more as you see the day approaching".

I beseech everyone to support someone to do good work because your availability to support others is the best gift of hospitality for the mission and purpose of God.

Walking by faith and hearing the word of God built my family and I. The scripture says in John 1:12, "As many as received Him, to them He gave the right to become children of God, to those who believe in His name."

From the day I became born again, I strived to be perfect in my daily walk with God. My main goal was to pursue the power of the Holy Spirit.

Romans 10:10, "For it is by believing in your heart that you are made right with God, and it is by confessing that you are saved."

This declaration raised my spirits up: 1st John 4:3 says, "Every spirit that does not confess that Jesus Christ has come in flesh is not of God. And this is the spirit of the antichrist which you have heard was coming, and now already in the world."

The word impacted me, and I continued to meditate on it.

B. My Thirst

My conversion was linked to the obedience, and practice of the Word of God that I heard from preaching and I read in my own devotion.

This scripture, 2 Chronicles 7: 14-16, says "If my people who are called by My Name will humble themselves and pray and seek My Face, and turn their wicked ways, then I will hear from

Heaven and will forgive their sin and heal their land. Now My Eyes will be open and My Ears attentive to the prayer made in this place. For now, I have chosen and sanctified this house and that My name may be there forever, and My eyes and my heart will be there perpetually".

I rejected all things standing as idols in my life, and I pressed on towards my goal to grow deeper, and know the divine trinity personally.

I wanted God to hear my prayers. I searched my heart, and everything around me that could hinder my prayers from being uprooted. I went on to plant new seeds of truth, and I decided to walk out my salvation not to fall into the hands of the antichrist.

It is not easy walking in the Lord. Sometimes I would fall back, but then I would get back and I would quickly repent. I'm now strongly rooted and grounded in the love of God, Jesus Christ, and my Redeemer.

The only thing you need is obedience to the Word of God and commitment. I have been healed from curses, condemnation, brokenness, accusations and lies of the enemy.

The good news is, I was saved at the time when I was very depressed with family issues. Come to the fountain, to the river's source, and you will never be thirsty. The word of Truth is the fountain; the word of eternal life, which speaks and confesses the truth.

C. The Outcome of Good Confession

Turn to God when you are lost.

I was lost in my sins and trespasses, but when I made up my mind to follow and obey the word of God, things turned for my good. I had an altar for God at my house; it was revered as a place for prayer.

I abstained from drinking alcohol, and I told no lies as I devoted my entire life to pleasing God. Our house was dedicated to God, so I could not allow alcoholic drinks on my living table.

One day, I received our pastors as visitors in my house. We all sat down, chatted, but I didn't share any alcoholic drink. Then, I opened our cabinet that was filled with different bottles of wine and whisky. Our pastors were more than speechless. They gave us some scriptures which helped us understand and get knowledge, because people perish for lack of knowledge.

There is power in the word of God. Do not be discouraged by circumstances; find spiritual food in the word. The word of God is the fountain of life - Meditate on his word. Proverbs 20:1 says, "Wine is a mocker, strong drink is a brawler, and whosoever is led astray by it is not wise".

As I continually looked unto God's word, I realised there was no way I could ever go back to my old ways.

Find a word to feed yourself, and you will begin to see the goodness of the Maker of Heaven and Earth in your life. Always continue to read and meditate on God's word to recover all your blessings.

I questioned myself- "Am I a king or a queen that I should stop drinking?" The answer came to me in Revelation 1: 5-6, which says: "From Jesus Christ, the faithful witness, the firstborn from the dead, and the ruler over the kings of the earth to Him who loved us and washed us from our sins in His own blood and has made us kings and priests to His God and Father to Him be glory dominion forever and ever."

Also, Ephesians 5:18 says, "Don't be drunk with wine, because that will ruin your life. Instead, be filled with the Holy Spirit."

I used to drink alcohol a lot, and when I would wake up in the morning after an alcohol drinking spree, I would have terrible headaches and feel very tired. The solution was to let go and never again drink alcohol.

Why do you spend money and wages on what is not bread and does not satisfy? We must learn to eat what is good, and let our soul delight itself in abundance.

Isaiah 55:2 says, "Incline your ear, and comes to Me, hear, your soul shall live; and I will make an everlasting covenant with you". Since it was God's command, everyone at home understood why we had to stop drinking.

My husband took all the bottles and gave them to some friends, and the leftovers were thrown in bins. There was one full bottle of wine left that He tried to give to my son, but my son refused and said, "No, it is a cursed drink. I can't drink it". By meditating on God's word regularly, we were saved from drinking alcoholic drinks.

It got to a point where I started to feel sick whenever I came across shops selling alcohol. Even if they were offering free bottles of wine, I didn't look at them.

Later in life, I visited a family who offered me a drink. Unknown to me, it had a bit of alcoholic content in it. I drank the drink offered to me without knowing, but then I started vomiting because of the alcoholic content, which I genuinely did not know it had.

The Holy Spirit took control of my heart, mind, body, and directed my steps in the process. No one else has been able to change my behaviour since then.

We should learn to drink from the fountain of life and be submissive to our maker. We should employ God's word to renew our strength, and overcome the challenges against our destines. I got back my life through the grace of God.

There is no time wasted in humbling, and disciplining ourselves for a good diet needed for spiritual growth. We must eat milk and solid food; and also feed ourselves spiritually.

Likewise, if we expect to see great miracles, we must put in the work. The prerequisite is to search our hearts and be converted from things that will destroy our destiny. We must make declarations and decide to stick to the vows we made, and also act with faith.

The just shall live by faith and walk in Spirit, not by sight.

D.   Hold on to Grace

At a time, I found myself powerless as I was carrying shopping bags. My body began to ache from all the heavy lifting of bags filled with groceries. I lived in a big town where everyone minded their business, and rarely offered to help anyone.

On that fateful day, everyone was rushing to fulfil their own duties, and no one offered me a lift. I said to myself, "I must come out from this burden". I prayed, "Lord, help me to pass my driving test and get my licence."

At the age of fifty-three, people despised me because I could not pass the United Kingdom driving test for a license. I decided to learn driving intensively. The instructor would tell me, "Oh no, you can't pass. Keep practising.", but I told him, "Please stop, do not tell me negative things because I will pass my test."

But God is good!

I became stronger, and I was able to accomplish my work, and follow up on the education of my children. My hand was healed from all the failures, and stress of my daily life. If you put your trust in God and in His Mighty Power, and do not lean on to your own understanding, God will answer you in due time. Those who wait upon the Lord do not lose anything.

Hold on to the Grace of God, and you will prosper in everything your hands find to accomplish.

I memorised the whole of Psalms 23. It became my confession every morning till today. Truly, the Lord is my shepherd, and I shall not be in want. He makes me lay down in the green pastures.

We shall speak positive affirmations into our life, and not allow any situation to move us out of the sight of our dreams. From time to time, I learnt to be free from negative thoughts, and I was able to cast out bad habits, likewise lies. No matter the problems we face, Jesus has overcome them all.

John 16:33 says "In the world you will have tribulation, but be of good cheer, I have overcome".

I also learned not to be ruled by anger. When we frequently give anger a chance to feaster, it disconnects us from God. Be mindful of having any malicious behaviour that might lead you to sin. Do not let the sun go down on your wrath.

Ephesians 4:26-27 further says "An angry person upsets everyone around them and they make serious mistakes as a result."

I learned to be satisfied and grateful. There was a time, when I did not have enough clothes to go to church with. Some people asked me, "Why don't you dress nicely? You need to buy smart clothes." I simply told them my time had not come yet. Now I have more than enough, and more.

Be thankful to God and be happy with humility, because God will lift you up in due season. Sometimes, I see gifts coming from different sisters, brothers and children, and I am just grateful to God. You only need to let God fight for you, and you shall keep the peace.

Do not look down for help in any situation; instead look up unto God and wait patiently unto The Creator of Heaven and

Earth for help.

Once you have received Christ Jesus into your life, your entire life will be transformed, and you will go from grace to grace, and from glory to glory. Do not miss your opportunity to realign your life with God. Call upon Him, and He will answer you because He is your father. Renew your strength, and put your trust in Him.

Indeed, when you speak to God, know that you are talking to your Father because it says those who have received Christ Jesus as the Lord, to them He has given them the right to become children of God. We speak to our Father and the Almighty God. If you are still doubting, ask God to reveal himself to you, and the Holy Spirit will empower you.

I was lost and stuck to another religion I knew of in primary school, but I have never had complete joy until I confessed, and received Christ Jesus as My personal Lord and My Saviour.

You have to remove yourself from any bondage or any form of slavery, and be on a focused path led by Jesus Christ. The wide way leads to depletion, but the narrow way leads to eternal and everlasting life.

You might have heard many stories; but you have to taste the Love of God yourself, and see the miracles to truly understand what I'm talking about, because the One in us is greater than the one of the World.

Our lives are tested because we each have glorious destines. The Word says, no weapon formed against you will prosper, for this is the heritage of children of God.

E. Passion to Speak the Name of Jesus

I am passionate about doing the Will of God, telling others about salvation, and being compassionate to help others. We know that God rewards all the works we do for others.

I learned not to envy because where enviousness exists, confusion and evil things are imminent. I decided to stop being depressed because bitterness burns away our body; consumes and cuts off the blessings from God.

The Holy Spirit had set me free, and the result was that God had given me a Spirit of thankfulness, praise, and worship. In all that I did, I refused to be hopeless.

In whatever I needed to do; I would put my trust in God. I prayed the Holy Spirit would lead me right.

I was not afraid to do work, as I knew God was with me, and his angels were around me. With God, all things are possible to those who believe. I have been working, and I have been able to support my orphans and survivors of genocide with faith, for I found grace and favour with men everywhere I stepped in. The Grace of God is available to those who put their trust and hope in the Maker, Creator of Heaven and Earth.

How did I work and remain full of energy to overcome all the side effects of the genocide I went through?

I loved this Word of God and employed it in all situations. Isaiah 40:29-31, "He gives power to the weak people, and to those who have no might He increases strength. Even the youths shall faint and weary, and the young men utterly fall. But those who wait on the Lord shall renew their strength; they shall mount up with wings like eagles. They shall run and not be weary, they shall walk and not faint."

It is our decision to engage in obedience, commitment, dedication, and to walk into our blessings. Call upon God, Lord Jesus and the Holy Spirit for everything you find to do, for this is the mystery of the secret in our life.

I developed many skills to do my work. Above all, I received the gifts of the Holy Spirit and the fruits of love, joy, peace, patience, kindness, gentleness, faithfulness, humility, and self-control; to enjoy my lifestyle and welcome everyone in need into my home. We accommodated different girls in need. Some were even addicted to alcohol and smoking.

One girl was converted to Christ's Kingdom, and began prospering well in her academy. The Lord says: "Come to me you who weary, I will give you rest." She is now a woman of prayer; a loving, kind, and wonderful mother.

My dearest reader, I employ you to open your heart and bless somebody in need. Our house is the house of solutions, and the uncomforted will find comfort in your premises.

You are gifted to use your talents to bring hope to the hopeless. Salvation goes with fruitfulness. Apply the Word in your life and wait upon the Lord for answers, knowing daily that the Truth fights for your victory.

I encourage everyone to seek God first, and other things will come in abundance. You have been blessed to be a blessing on to others.

In the world, you will have tribulations. You will overcome all, and be a witness to the goodness of the Lord. When you feel discouraged by circumstances, remember Apostle Paul saying, "I have learned in whatever state I am to be content".

I was rescued and saved, so I can tell you how I overcame, and how I live in the Kingdom of God. The word of our mouth and from our heart is our source of victory, or failure. The Truth that fought yesterday, today, and tomorrow will remain the same for all generations.

The song, "Passion" by Glorious Day reminds me always of my salvation. Looking back, I spent many years living in the world, following the lusts of my flesh or just copying what my other friends were doing. I had a difficult life, and was saved at the age of fifty-three. Please do not waste your life.

Come to the Lord, you will be rescued and saved from perishing. Heaven is real, and hell is real. Believe in Christ, the source of the unperishable fountain from the river of life.

Chapter 10
Redeemed Back to Life

"And the God of all the grace, who called you to his eternal glory in Christ, after you have suffered a little while, will restore you and make you strong, firm and steadfast."
- 1st Peter 5:10

The work of restoration can't begin until a problem is fully faced."
- Dan Allender.

You must know God blesses those who seek Him diligently, and those who know their God; shall do exploits.

"If you diligently heed the voice of the Lord your God, and do what is right in His sight, give ear to His commandment and keep all His statutes, I will put none of the diseases on you which I have brought on the Egyptians. For I am the Lord who heals." - Exodus 15:26

1. Recovering Sight

When we humble ourselves and repent of our sins, God hears us and heals our land.

Deuteronomy 23:14 says, "For the Lord your God walks during your camp, to deliver you and to give your enemies over to you; therefore, your camp shall be holy, that He may see no unclean thing among you, and turn away from you". Let us continually stay in God's presence so our land is restored.

I was sick and I knew my eyesight was not good. I was living without properly taking care of myself because of the trauma from 1994 genocide. A special friend invited me to her house, as she had a visitor who was Prophetess Faith. She was dedicated to serving the Lord, and reaching out to many souls.

On my way, the Prophetess told the gathered audience she saw me in her spiritual vision. The Prophetess said, "Here is the woman I saw in my vision". She prayed for me and said, "You woman, you don't sleep". I responded and told her "No".

My sleep was always interrupted by small noises, and I would jump out from fear to wake up. She prophesied into my life "From now, you will sleep well" – and till today, I sleep at night like a baby.

As a survivor of genocide, it was either I could not sleep well enough, or I would jump from the fear of explosions of grenades caused by the genocide. The trauma led to insomnia from 1994 to 2011.

We should never despise invitations to hear the word of God, because the invitation is from the Lord, hence we should listen and obey.

Once I knew this, I embraced this in my heart and I was motivated to attend gospel conferences. During a preaching and prayer intercession session, the prophetess came to me and grabbed my glasses, she proceeded to throw it in the air.

The atmosphere was electric and I could feel the Holy Spirit moving. Instantly, I began to scream to myself that I was healed of whatever sickness that was in my body. I asked myself, "At my old age, how can this woman touch my face and throw my glasses away like that?"

I figured out much later the touch was necessary for my healing. I declared that I received my miracles for new visions. The power of God filled the atmosphere; and many people fell on the floor.

The following week, I went to the medical centre for a routine check-up. When I was about to leave, I felt something in my right eye. The doctor examined my eyes and urgently referred me to the Eye Hospital.

A few days later, I received a letter that said I needed minor surgery. From time to time, I would have visions that were doubled. God was with me through all this.

The Surgeon examined me and said I needed an MRI Scan

urgently. Eventually, I was diagnosed with "Tear Gland Right Swelling".

The doctor was very kind and patient with me. After passing all the pre-op assessments, I had the operation on my eye and the swelling tear gland was removed.

In the theatre room, before the surgery, I asked doctors to let me pray, and I promised God, "If you restore my sight, I will tell the world what you have done for me". I fell down on my knees and prayed. "Please heal me and restore my sight, and I will use my sight to tell the people the good news of the gospel."

The operation started at nine o'clock in the morning, and I woke up at three o'clock in the afternoon. The tear gland was taken out, I never had double vision again and my mouth was restored to its proper position.

Sister Elizabeth was always driving me to the Manchester Infirmary Royal Hospital in the United Kingdom during all my assessments and treatments, and she helped me understand the medical technicalities involved. She continued to come to my house to help me with prayers and encouragement.

I urge that when it is possible for us, we should try to respond to the invitation of the gospel for any blessed gathering; have your own expectation, and you will see what is available for you.

I was once blind, but now I can see. I was lost, but now I am found.

Be available to listen to God with your heart. We should do His will, fear Him, love Him and serve him.

I praise God for this miraculous healing, for if it had stayed longer, it could have resulted in a cancerous disease. I encourage you, whenever things are hard, no matter the environment you find yourself, go on your knees and speak to God. His arms are always opened to us. Make a vow and honour it, and you will prosper. The power of healing is in the Name of Jesus Christ.

Emotional, financial, spiritual, and physical healing can be found in the name of Jesus. Our conversion to God brought us many blessings. We were able to walk in our God-given destines, and be more valuable to ourselves and others. We consistently used the word of God to overcome all challenging situations, and to change things to have a better life pleasing our Father.

This scripture says in Ephesians 6:14-17, "Stand therefore, having girded your waist with truth, having put on the breastplate of righteousness. Having shod your feet with the preparation of the gospel of peace; above all, take the shield of faith which you will be able to quench all the fiery darts of the wicked one. And take the helmet of salvation and the sword of the Spirit, which is the word of God."

We are called to be strong, to watch and pray to God the Father, "Praying always with all supplications in the Spirit, being watchful to the end with perseverance and supplication for all the saints" —Ephesians 6:18

From my experience in the 1994 genocide, I couldn't stop speaking to God every day and night. I learnt that we are fighting against the forces of hell, invisible powers, unseen satanic structures, and satanic forces. It is not by our might, neither by our strength but by the Spirit, says the Lord.

The situations are subject to change when we apply the word of God with faith in our lives. If our hearts are clean, and are thoughts are aligned with his, then God will hear us. Where is the word? The word is in our tongue, and the Bible.

2. The Word is our Sword

The word says in Isaiah 55:11, "So shall My word be that goes forth from my mouth; it shall not turn to Me void, but it shall accomplish what I please. And it shall prosper in the thing for which I send it.".

We have been called for a purpose and have been elected to do good works. We are a chosen generation and a special people. 1st Peter 2:9 says, "But you are a chosen generation, a royal priesthood, a holy people, that you may proclaim the praises of

Him who called you out of darkness into His marvellous light".

Some time ago, I accompanied a friend of mine; who has now become a lawyer to the magistrate court. The allegations against her were false as the leader wanted to cover up for his mistakes. This leader bribed the staff to testify against this innocent sister of mine.

At the court, all the witnesses began to give their account of the particular case. I kept praying within me "Oh God! Have mercy, Lord. Fight for your daughter and let the enemy be scattered and confused. Let there be a revelation of the truth". I knew my sister would not tell lies to cover up for herself, as she was a godly woman who feared the Lord.

The last person testified and gave the true full details of the incidents, thereby wiping away all the wrong accusations. The audience were more than speechless after they heard the truth. The accuser; likewise the false witnesses, were confused and put to shame. The accuser was dismayed and embarrassed before the judges. My sister pled not guilty, and no condemnation was laid upon her.

The word is the sword of the Spirit, searching into the deepest parts of men to drill and expose hidden things to the audience. My sister was restored and healed, and she kept on reciting Exodus 14: 14 which says "The Lord God will fight for you, and you shall keep your peace."

I went to look after a person that was on a sick bed. There was a particular period when he began to have seizures regularly. I started to call upon the name of the Lord on his behalf. I would say, "Be healed in the Name of Jesus. Spirit of death, I command you to go in Jesus' name".

The doctor and staff nurses came urgently to rescue him, but the man was already breathing fine. Then he said loudly, "You woman, thank you for your prayer. You saved me". I told him the glory wasn't mine because it belonged to God.

The doctor replied him asking, "What about me? - I don't deserve any glory?". But the man remained silent, and just kept rejoicing.

The power of restoration is in the word of your mouth. I visited a close friend who was also like a sister to me, she had cancer and we kept praying and speaking the word of God to heal her completely. I encouraged her to go for a prayer session.

She rose up and attended the prayer session with faith. Everything changed for her that same evening, and she got healed. She is a living testimony.

When we speak good words, we bring life; and when we speak bad words, we pronounce curses. Many people are living under curses due to the word spoken in their lives.

3. Bondage to Freedom

A young girl devoted to Christ was invited to preach in a church. Walking to the altar of God, a woman leader saw her and turned her face to the wall until the preaching was over. The young preacher became discouraged and dwelt on the unpleasant memory of being rejected by a woman in the church.

The rejection lingered in her mind, so much so that she refused every invitation presented to her to preach again, for she was scared to stand before the congregation that despised her.

Then, she received the word of God in Joshua 1:9, saying, "Have I not commanded you? Be strong and of good courage do not be afraid, nor be dismayed, for the Lord your God is with you wherever you go".

I keep encouraging everyone not to fear rejection, instead be courageous and speak the word over your life. Revival and restoration are the fruits of the words we hear and believe.

How did I get healed? I made a decision to surrender my life to God. I willingly asked Lord Jesus to come into my heart and my life.

The word transformed my life and through this word, I turned away from my old bad ways and learnt new habits to please God.

My conversion to Christ has led me to overcome any situation and has healed me from psychological trauma, curses over my life, and broken chains. The essential remedy is our confession that God sent the Messiah Jesus not to condemn us, but to give eternal life.

I came to know the Lord intimately when I was fifty-three years old, and I realised I wasted my life following evil spirits. If you can read this message, arise and shine; and let the Lord be the master of your life.

In these end times, please teach your children how they should grow. Mass media corrupts people and makes them perish for lack of knowledge. Psalm 127: 6 says, "Train up a child in the way he should go, and when he is old, he will not depart from it".

All teaching and communication tools are available to save people from living failures, curses, and psychological trauma. Sicknesses and diseases are curable from words of our mouth.

The restoration requires walking with God in obedience to what He says. For ages, those who lived according to what God says have been counted as righteous people.

James 5:16-18 says, "Confess your trespasses to one another, and pray to one another, that you may be healed, the effective fervent prayer of the righteous man avails much".

Elijah was a man with a nature like ours, he prayed earnestly that it would not rain, and it did not rain on the land for three years and six months. He prayed again, and the heaven gave rain, and the earth produced its fruits.

My personal trauma affected me to the point that I avoided meeting any Rwandan diaspora abroad, and I refused to go back to my own country, but now I know that, my return was essential to my healing.

I returned to Rwanda for the first time in 13 years, and I counted it to be the best time for my reunification with them. I did not know how much I had missed the cultural tradition, dance and my fellow compatriots.

I received a special welcome back address from everyone, even from the immigration staff at the airport, from family, and friends. I felt loved and healed.

My healing required me to go back to where I was wounded and see God's goodness. I love my original homeland Rwanda, and the United Kingdom; who accepted me just the way I was.

I met Jesus, my life changed, and I went from glory to glory. I made prayers of repentance and forgiveness, and my chains were broken forever.

It says in Isaiah 28:5, "In that day the Lord of hosts will be for a crown of glory and diadem of beauty to the remnant of His people"

Instead of harbouring stress, shame, disappointment, failure, and trauma; we are to seek the Lord God, who holds the key for us to be restored and healed.

Every valley has been exalted, and every mountain and hill has been brought down, and the crooked places have been made straight for God's glory.

I always put God in everything I do. I constantly proclaim that I am healed and restored.

Chapter 11
New Life, New Living

Before we were in the womb, God knew us, ordained us, and sanctified us.

> "Before I formed you in the womb, I knew you before you were born, I sanctified you; I ordained you a prophet to the nation"
> - Jeremiah 1: 5

He has a plan of good, and not a plan of evil for us. Even when we are old, we will be fruitful and be flourishing like a palm tree.

> "For I know the thought that I think toward you, says the Lord, thoughts of peace and not of evil, to give you a future and a hope."
> - Jeremiah 29:11

This is the confidence we have been created for good and to live according to His will.

1.   The Past and the Quest to Serve
Try to analyse your past, and you will figure out your reason to live.

I was brought up in a Catholic school.

My Grandmother became sick, and refused to go to the hospital. Gradually, I saw the signs that she was going to die. From my Christian knowledge, I remembered we needed to bring a priest to give her the last benediction.

As a young teenager, I told my uncle with determination to quickly bring the priest before she drew her last breath. My uncle looked at me and said "Let us go, you little girl".

I went with my uncle to invite the priest to our home; to pray and anoint my grandmother. I used to share a bed with her, but after the exercise I decided to sleep on a mat placed next to her bed.

At this point, she could not talk, rather she was using her fingers as a means of communication. She kept pointing to a particular spot, but alas I couldn't figure out what she was trying to say. Much to my displeasure, she passed away after a long struggle. I am assured my grandmother went to heaven to meet Jesus Christ.

It is very good to put our children in good Christian schools, for they will be taught godly lessons that will save them from hell. In my stay at the university, the religious sister trained me to join the church choir as a member.

Every Sunday, my adopted parents who also happen to be pastors (Kayijuka and Rose) always made sure that we all, as one family, participated in the attendance of the Mass Service.

After I got married, I backslid and stopped following the way of the Lord. I was addicted to work and caring after my family. I was very active in the world, following the lust of flesh, and the lust of my eyes. My late husband would pray before sleeping, and in the morning before leaving for work. I just observed and did not follow in his good example.

The call of God can never perish, as there was a day I walked to the house of God, I felt His power upon me, and got arrested by the Holy Spirit.

My late husband, and myself became members of the Catholic Church. We were also active choir members, as we loved praising and worshipping the Lord. We were then paired up with my friend to organise a prayer group, and the gathering was to be held either in my house or my friend's house.

This scripture shows us this, Isaiah 49:1-2, The Lord has called Me from the womb, from the matrix of my mother He has made mention of my name. He has made my mouth like a sharp sword; in the shadow of His Hand, He has hidden Me, and made Me a polished shaft; in His quiver He has hidden Me".

Be encouraged to use the gift of God deposited in you to the glory of his name.

The struggle during the genocide inspired me to be prepared to go to heaven, and not to rot in Hell. I encouraged my late husband, Joseph Nyagatare, to baptize all our children and among them - David Ricardo died within that period.

A member of the choir was used by God to assist in our escape through a transport escort. This was just a few minutes before we were almost killed during the Genocide crisis in Rwanda.

It is therefore recommended for everyone to find a fellowship group that will help assist you to spiritually grow.

Fellowshipping with God fearing people opened my eyes to appreciate the essence of my life here on earth. Someone will be your stepping-stone to victory in the presence of your enemies. Therefore, endeavour not to undermine any age group of men, or women you come across in life.

God called us long time ago for our own benefit. When you critically examine your life story, you will discover as an individual that God has been faithful in various ways, because of his unusual moves to rescue you from destruction. His grace for the purpose of our life is unquestionable. He is standing at the door, waiting for you to yield to His will and His voice.

There was a time in my life when I worked for The Salvation Army

Homeless Centre. Majority of residents had various needs and had to be supported. They were homeless men; some enmeshed in alcoholic, some addicted to drugs, there were also refugees, and released prisoners — all looking for accommodation.

The Salvation Army had set up prayer times during our break and everyone including staff and resident members, were free to participate. I volunteered to take over and lead prayer service whenever the chaplain was off duty.

The residents were very good, and for nine years nobody misbehaved or showed any form of animosity to me. We often looked at biblical scriptures together, and I ministered to those willing to listen.

I came to discover that I was called a long time ago, but I ignored the instructions from the Holy Spirit. In my heart, I was not living like Jesus who was the perfect model in depicting love, humility, faithfulness, obedience, and sacrifice.

Look through your past stories, and you will find the call of God in your life at several intervals in your life.

No matter the situation, I genuinely loved to help and protect the vulnerable. Have we bothered to ask ourselves why we have escaped numerous dangers, such as car accidents, killings, sicknesses, and many more?

All that happens should be seen as marks of testing because we are carriers of great destinies, and the devil will always want to obstruct our glorious destinies. Good times and bad times are life teaching events, all created to renew our strength. The Will of God is that we shall prosper as our soul prospers for His glory.

I found out my call is to tell others my testimonies and employ the word of God in lives, as the only truth that fights for sure victory. For the word of God is a lamp to our feet and a light to our path (Psalms 119: 105). Without words of encouragement, we are lost in the world and we are nothing.

We should build our life upon God, who is our rock; for other gods are sinking sand. Psalms 127:1, says "Unless the Lord builds the house, they labour in vain who builds it. Unless the Lord guards the city, the watchman stays awake in vain.

You are born with talents and gifts to be used to glorify the Maker of the Heavens and Earth; instead of your own glory. If you have the gift of teaching, you are called to teach the word to the lost to have the bread of life. If you are good in leading people, it means you are called to be a good leader. If you are good in hospitality, it means you have the gift of hospitality.

The Bible commands us to submit to God, and the devil will flee away from us. We should not bury our talents and gifts, but instead we should use them with wisdom and to glorify the

Almighty God.

If you are good singer, you are called to sings praises and worship unto God. If you are good in looking after children, it means you are called to minister to the children. If you are good in giving advice, you are called to be a counsellor for the Lord.

Without God in the equation, the achievement would only last for a short period of time and end in disaster. Today, I encourage everyone to take advantage of good times and bad times to discover the call of God.

2.   The Availability of Grace

Romans 5:1-2 says, "Therefore, having been justified by faith, we have peace with God through our Lord Jesus Christ. Through whom also we have access by faith into His grace in which we stand, and rejoice in hope of the glory of God."

By the special grace of God, I was elected to be ordained as a Deaconess in the Church of God referred to as Arise and Shine Christian Ministries in Manchester, United Kingdom.

One student I met, who used to be addicted to drinking alcohol and smoking drugs was transformed. She became born again, then she converted to Christianity wholeheartedly. She became a very fervent Christian and finished her studies with success.

We are called to use our blessings and wisdom from God to help others to enjoy the goodness of the Lord. The Truth will fight for us in every situation and we shall keep our peace.

I urge those that have received this message to take a stand, and ask God to strengthen them in their ministries. I would love to encourage everyone to give their life to Jesus Christ and receive Him into their hearts. He is the excellent shepherd, the way, the truth and the life.

I moved from glory to the glory, and I was ordained as an Evangelist in the Church; New Life International church in Manchester, United Kingdom. With God, we are able to do the best because we are no longer alone, we have extra power to enable us to fulfil our destiny.

1st John 4:4 says, "Little children, you are from God and have overcome them, for he who is in you is greater than he who is in the world".

We have the Spirit of God in us to instruct us in the way we should go, and things we should do for the glory of our Heavenly Father.

"Who shall separate us from the love of Christ? Shall tribulation, or distress, or persecution, or famine, or nakedness, or danger, or sword? None; In all things we are more than conquerors"
- Romans 8:35-37

3.   Race of Wisdom to Live

My new resolution is to tell others about Jesus Christ. My goal is to encourage myself and others to have the word of God in their life. There is power in our tongue to give life or to kill. Remember, if you confess with your mouth that Jesus is the lord and believe in your heart that God raised Him from the dead, you will be saved (Romans 10:8-9).

The Lord says blessed are the peacemakers for they shall be called the Sons of God.

A.   Talking positively and rejecting all confusion.

For God did not give us the spirit of confusion, but of love and discernment of spirits.

I have learned to be free from negative emotions, bad habits, lies, and anxiousness. No matter what problems we have in life, we are overcomers. John 16:33, "In the world you will have tribulation, but be of good cheer, I have overcome the world".

We must constantly meditate on His promises and walk with the Lord, because every situation comes to either strengthen or to weaken us. Therefore, we must not lose courage, and we must focus on what the word says by looking unto Jesus the author of our faith.

As a new creation in Christ, I always made sure to put God first; and ask His Will to be done. One day, I booked a flight to travel with my family and when we arrived at the airport, the checking attendant announced my flight was scheduled for another date. It was not good news as I was going back to school with the children.

I did not understand because I had the flight ticket that said my flight was scheduled for that particular day. I started praying, and a relative that accompanied me to the airport asked the team if there was anything that could be done.

Few minutes later, I saw someone running to us to check in all our luggage. Clearly, the plane could not leave without us. Everyone was mobilised to help us through all the checking requirements.

When we finally entered, the passengers and hostesses were angry as to why we had been waiting for long.

I now always say to myself when there is a problem, "Knock on the door, and it shall be opened; Ask and it shall be given to you, seek and you will find"

I used to work night shifts, and I started a prayer chain during my night shift; which a lot of people engaged in. It wasn't only to my own benefit, but also for my colleagues and patients benefit.

I worked long shifts both during the day and at night, but I would always finish the duty joyfully because the Joy of the Lord was my strength. People would ask me "How do you do it?". They couldn't believe because of my fragile age. I would tell them in return that it was just my new life in Christ strengthening me.

B. The Daily Watchword.

Prayer time is vital for all of us to live a worthy life.

We enjoy the goodness of God because of the prayers and intercession made on behalf for mankind. We should pray in any opportunity we find: in the morning, afternoon, and at evening. The Bible commands us to pray without ceasing.

Setting time to study the word of God is very important; likewise asking the Holy Spirit for spiritual direction.

I can't count how many times I have prayed in the day because I encountered unexpected challenges. I have learnt to talk to my Father whenever I'm in a fix, because He hears me. He said, "In time of trouble, call upon Me and I will answer you and show thee signs of good, so your enemy will be ashamed.

Isaiah 41:10 says, "Fear not for I am with you; be not dismayed, for I am your God. I will strengthen you. Yes, I will help you. I will uphold you with my righteous hand". Also, 2 Corinthians

5:17 says, "Therefore, if anyone is in Christ, he is a new creation, old things have passed away; behold, all things have become new".

I have always loved to teach children about the word of God, so when they grow up; they will be strong in wisdom, knowledge, and understanding.

These children are now able to stand before any congregation, and speak with confidence. They can tell their testimonies, and motivate people to attend Sunday service.

I encourage everyone to not hesitate to lead someone to Christ the saviour. We are saved to help others to be saved. We have the power, the grace, and mercy of God to achieve our goals.

We no longer waver in thoughts and actions, but we follow instructions from what God has said about us. We know that in Romans 8:2, "For the law of the spirit in Christ Jesus has made me free from the law of sin and death".

We shall no longer be regarded as children tossed around, and carried about with every doctrine, or by the trickery of men. The new wisdom of life requires us to have mercy for others and win souls for Christ.

Say this prayer of Salvation with someone who is willing to have God in their life:

"Oh God, forgive me of my sins. I believe that the Lord Jesus Christ died for me. Dear Lord Jesus, come into my heart and I give my life to You. Thank You for being my Lord and my saviour".

For sure, there is a joy and celebration in Heaven for a soul saved. Those committed with faith will have a special feeling of intense peace, because they have received the Spirit of God within them.

"Do not remember the former thing, not consider the things of old." - Isaiah 43:18

We are to remember the ministry of reconciliation and have confidence in the truth."

"Now all things are of God who has reconciled us to Himself through Jesus Christ, He has given us the ministry of reconciliation" - 2 Corinthians 5: 18-20

The ministry of reconciliation is to announce the message of what God has done in atoning for our sins. Those already reconciled have the commission to bring the message to others.

God was in Christ and reconciled the world to Himself, not imputing their trespasses against them.

The new life we live in Christ requires us to discipline ourselves. I have learned this word and it changed me because of the promises embedded in the scripture, Romans 8:1, says," There is therefore now no condemnation to those who are in Christ Jesus, who do not walk according to the flesh, but to the spirit."

My past is over and the new things have come. My new life is to be led by the power of God with humility, and submission. For, we are to submit to God and resist the devil.

Humility goes before honour, and pride goes before destruction. Choose honour and reject destruction through the obedience to the Word of God. I learned to listen to God, and to ask for direction.

Are we peacemakers or troublemakers? This question should continually probe our minds. Are we building good relationships with people around us, or are we destroying them by speaking, cursing, or teaching false doctrines?

My new life commands me to put off fleshly desires and live according to what God says. We should allow the Spirit of God; the Holy Spirit, the Spirit of Life, the Spirit of Adoption - to have dominion in our entire lives.

I have learned from Romans 8:8, that those who are in flesh cannot please God.

"For if you live according to the flesh you will die; but if by the spirit you put to death the deeds of the body, you will live. For as many as are led by the spirit of God are Sons of God."

- Romans 8:13-14

Therefore, we are encouraged, not to live according to the flesh but put to death the vulnerability of lusts in our bodies. The more people are led by the spirit, the more obedient they will be to God's word, and be conformed to His holy standards.

New life comprises of the commitment, self-discipline, and self-control of the entire work we are called to do. Without the spirit of life, we would find ourselves lost in flesh and unending disaster.

For the spirit of Christ, the spirit of the resurrection, and the spirit of God produced in us are essential spirits to have in our calling. Fulfilling God's plan depends on the fruits of the spirit in our life. Galatians 5:22 speaks about the fruits of the sprit which are; love, joy, peace, patience, kindness, goodness, faithfulness, gentleness, and self-control.

3. Lean on the Will of God

We shall walk in Spirit and in Truth, not to fulfil the desires of our bodies. For the will of God is that none shall perish, but shall have Eternal Life.

Only the Holy Spirit can produce these fruits in our lives. When the Spirit fully controls the lives of believer, they produce all these graces in their lives. God can never change, because He is trustworthy, loving, kind, compassionate, faithful, and merciful.

We should not be blinded by our sight, but we should open our hearts to receive the armour of God for Eternal life. We know all things work together for our good to those who love God; to those who are called according to His purpose (Romans 8:28). In all circumstances, I have always found new opportunities for unseen victories.

Indeed, we are blessed to be a blessing. What you have today is for God's glory, and it shall be honoured as we dedicate ourselves unto the Lord.

Isaiah 61:1, "The Spirit of the sovereign God is upon me because the Lord has anointed me to preach good news to the poor. He has sent me to bind up the broken hearted to proclaim freedom for the captives and release from darkness for the prisoners".

Spread the good news in every situation and let the Will of God be exalted. I have been working with many different and vulnerable people. God opened my eyes, and made me see he wanted me to be the vessel to lead them to Christ.

Have faith in Him, do the will of God; no one shall perish, but shall have eternal life.

Isaiah 52:7 says, "How beautiful upon the mountains are the feet of him who brings good news, who proclaims peace, who brings glad tidings of good things, who proclaims salvation, who says to Zion your God reigns".

We should ensure not to forgo the opportunity to consecrate, and dedicate our lives to God. I see God vested in all my situations; I look at everyone coming to me as God's sent.

Set down a time to pray, to search your heart, and to examine your entire life. Then, you will find what you have been called to do, and please God. It is never too late to wake up and enter into our destinies.

Chapter 12
Reject Lukewarmness

A wise man will hear and increase learning, and a man of
understanding will attain wise counsel.
– Faith Island Blog.

My complete healing, restoration, and daily victories are based
on God-given strategies.

I rejected lukewarmness, and focused on things that glorified
the Lord. Our attitude and our character have to look genuinely
unto God because He created us in His image, and gave us
dominion. One thing is to search our hearts, our attitudes, and
refuse any form of worldly corruption.

The Lord says in Isaiah 29:13, "These people come near to me
with their mouth and honour me with their lips, but their hearts
are far from me. Their worship of me is based on merely human
rules they have been taught".

Furthermore, the Lord also says in Revelation 3:15-16, "I know
your works, that you are neither cold or hot. I could wish you

were cold or hot. So then, because you are lukewarm, and neither cold or hot, I will vomit you out of my mouth".

From the day I heard this word, I looked to be hot for Christ and seek God. Jeremiah 6:16 amplifies this for it says, "Stand in the ways and see, and ask for the old paths, where the good way is, and walk in it; then you will find rest for your souls"

Faith is the master key to draw us closer to God; believing and trusting Him fully also guarantees us to draw closer to Him. For the Truth to fight, I had to know "to say no" to the things that were not honourable.

"Looking carefully lest anyone fall short of the grace of God; lest
any root of bitterness springing up cause trouble, and by this many
become defiled"
- Hebrews 12:55

A.   Faith is the Master Key

The principles of faith lead us to be joyful until the end of life here on earth. Hebrews 11:1 says "Now faith is the substance of the things hoped for, the evidence of the things not seen".

Also in Hebrews 11:6, "But without faith it is impossible to please Him, for he who comes to God must believe that He is the rewarder of those who diligently seek Him".

Faith is used by someone who has a firm and constant devotion to something to which he or she is united to, either by a promise or a pledge. The faithful is loyal and reliable. If you are faithful to someone or something, you remain loyal and keep the vows you made.

Your mind might be tempted to be corrupted with unlike minds. Therefore, we need to hear what builds up our spiritual life.

The Truth that fought for me, is the same truth that will fight for you to be anointed. Faith makes us to be like a tree planted by the rivers of water, that brings forth its fruits in its season, whose leaf also shall not wither.

We shall have faith in:

1.   *The knowledge in God's Character.*

> "For we walk by faith, not by sight"
> – 2 Corinthians 5:7

Faith is established in the knowledge of God, as we trust Him for understanding and wisdom in persecution. Understand that God calls His people to faithfulness, patience, and to never renounce faith in Jesus.

The genocide against the Tutsi in Rwanda around 1994, came

to an end because the fighters; Inkotanyi, had faith based on the truth to save the persecuted population of theTutsi. They knew the truth which was – God is always at the fore-front to defeat our enemies in order to complete healing.

"But without faith it is impossible to please Him, for he who comes to God must believe that He is, and that He is the rewarder of those who diligently seek Him".
- Hebrews 11:6

The spirit of the world is in opposition to God when we determine to stand in faith- Only then will the world lose the controlling influence it has over us. Practice the principles of faith-filled prayer, knowing that God will hear all your prayers that is in accordance with His will.

Be assured that victory is already yours in Christ.

"For with God, nothing is impossible".
- Luke 1:37

Faith in Christ and in the completed work of the cross allows a believer to endure rejection by the world and count all blessings from any reproach or suffering for the name of Jesus Christ. Have faith in God and the Lord Jesus Christ, lean not to your own understanding but ask the Holy Spirit to speak to you and guide you all in your ways.

2.   *Holding unto Jesus.*

In Mark 9:23, Jesus said, "If you believe, all things are possible to him who believe.

Faith accepts the Bible's record of who is Jesus, and what He has accomplished on our behalf. The believer accepts the benefits of Jesus' sacrifice, and enters God's presence with confidence.

The scripture says in Hebrews 12:2," Look unto Jesus, the author and finisher of our faith, who for the joy that was set before Him endured the cross, despising the shame, and has sat down at the right hand of the throne of God."

Faith is the willing to suffer with Christ, knowing you will receive a good reward. In many struggles I encountered, I strongly held on to my faith and I saw numerous rewards for it.

3.   *Choosing boldly and unswervingly*

Luke 1:37 "For with God, nothing will be impossible".

Hebrews 10:23 further says, "Let us hold fast the confession of our hope without wavering for He who promised, is faithful".

Faith is choosing boldly and unswervingly to believe what God has said. Faith freed me to live like never before for the good of others. Faith trained me to proclaim the gospel, and stand firm when tempted by unbelievers knowing God can do what He promised to do.

I learnt to believe we were also united with Jesus in His death, burial, and resurrection. My life has a lot of testimonies, so I live in a manner that helps to strengthen the faith of others.

I am learning my faith must believe and focus on proclaiming God's Word, without timidity and doubt. I steadfastly continue in faith, knowing nothing done in Jesus' name is in vain.

4.   *Believe God's word.*

Romans 10:17 says, "So then faith comes by hearing, and hearing by the word of God".

My faith chooses to believe God's word above my fears. Faith is not denying the circumstances; rather, it is in believing God's testimony and living in agreement with it. During the genocide in 1994, I was telling God all the time in persecutions that I was not going to die, but I would live.

The justification through laws or codes is impossible, because we are to receive God's gift of justification through faith in Christ Jesus.

I continued walking in faith ceaselessly, recognizing and believing in the certainty of my victory.

I read the scriptures daily to receive revelation of what God was telling me; and to find peace, joy, and faith. Faith believes absolutely in the divine inspiration of the Scriptures.

I was not frustrated by opposition, I just continued to stand strong, trusting God for His will to be accomplished upon my life. Be faithful in those things He has commissioned for you to do.

The scripture in Micah 7:7 says, "Therefore I will look to the Lord; I will wait for the God of my salvation; my God will hear me. To wait, tarry, hope, trust, expect, be patient and remain in anticipation for His mercy, and His rescue, His salvation".

I lived almost fifty-six days calling on to God for help, and I was rescued on the 2nd of June in 1994 by an army of strong forces that came to move me out of the pit.

When all the circumstances in our lives are painting negative pictures of failure, and loss; the natural reaction would be to complain, but rather this is the time to put our faith in God and in His Word.

I was grieving for twenty-six years, living with a broken heart because of the death of my first husband, my late son, and my in-laws in the 1994 genocide.

The government had built a very honourable memorial site for the 1994 genocide victims, but I couldn't resolve to move their bodies from the initial grave I made for them.

Through the unshakeable faith in God, I have been totally healed and persuaded to move their bodies to the memorial land set aside for victims from the 1994 genocide in Rwanda. I forgave myself completely and forgave all the génocidaires.

I hated people a lot because of the pain the world inflicted on me, but I found I was hurting myself and others with the hatred. With new found gladness and faithfulness, I decided to go to the funeral site of my late husband in 1994.

When we continually live in hurt and sorrow, we become like a man possessed by demons. I refused to dwell on the past, and I looked up to the Mighty God to be delivered from satanic bondage, and demonic strongholds.

With gladness and faithfulness, I decided to go to the funeral site of my beloved first late husband, and my late son.

5. *Seek first the things of God.*

Matthew 6:33, "But seek first the kingdom of God and His righteousness, and all these things shall come to you".

I am learning to make the work of God a priority, both with my time and with my possession. Gradually, I'm turning away from self-ambitions, and personal agenda to focus on advancing God's kingdom.

B.   Daily empowerment by the Holy Spirit.

"The secret of true happiness lies within unwavering devotion to God"
- Shri Radhe Maa

"You have to plan your devotion to God every day. And, the best time to plan it is before your day begins. If you don't plan it, your day will plan you. And so, I make a disciplined life of the study of the scriptures, reading the word every day"
- Ravi Zacharias.

The circumstances, tribulations, and duties in my life were always answered by prayers and supplication unto the Lord. I dedicated myself to God, and often I would fall from my steadfastness and from seeking God. Then, I would pick myself up and ask the Holy Spirit for strength and power to overcome all the terrible times.

Steps to getting empowered personally:
• Have a regular time to worship, to sing praises to the Lord, and to give love to Jesus Christ, God, and Holy Spirit.

- Repent quickly whenever the Spirit convicts us of sin.

- Gather often with God's people, and seek God diligently. Scripture says in Hebrews 13:15, "Therefore by Him let us continually offer the sacrifice of praise to God, that is the fruit of our lips, giving thanks to His name".

- Be diligent in attending Bible Study, and practice scripture memorization and meditation regularly. Let the Word in us offer praises to God and edify others. There was a time, I was sick and went to the hospital, but I couldn't speak. I could only pray quietly in my heart. I was saying the scriptures I had memorized, and few hours later, I recovered quickly and I was discharged to go home.

I came to know the journey with Christ involves a lot of sacrifices. I gave accommodation to some homeless people, in spite of their state and I had some challenges with my family. My family wasn't too pleased and felt I should not have given help to the homeless, because of their unpleasant lifestyle.

Nevertheless, I aimed to achieve the goal God had set for me by sparing no effort in pressing towards the mark of knowing Christ.

Chapter 13
The Word of Truth & the Strategies

"The wise are mightier than the strong, and those with knowledge
grow stronger and stronger"
- Proverbs 24:5

A Rwandan who has fully experienced the horror of the 1994
genocide, can easily be frustrated and distraught, whenever
there is a reminder of the holocaust. So, there is a need to grow
in the knowledge of the word of God to get freedom.

Take a stand and let the Truth fight; love everyone without
discrimination, and look for good will to prevail. Life in the
world is short but we have a destination, where we will live
eternally. This is the confidence that makes us pursuit the race
without looking back.

From generation to generation, we have testimonies due to our
obedience of commandments from the Lord God. We have
the warning of death or life. Therefore, He who has ears to hear,
let him hear.

The book of Mark 4: 11-12 says "To you it has been given to

know the mystery of the Kingdom of God but to those who are outside, all things come in parables, so that seeing they may see and not perceive, and hearing they may hear and not understand, lest they should turn to the lord and their sin be forgiven".

After thirteen years of being born again, I have come to understand the gospel of Jesus Christ. I questioned myself, "How can I keep this covenant and promise till my final destination?"

The important key is: How do we grow in godliness and holiness?

I used to cry to God, "Oh Lord, when will my blessing come" However, I heard back from the Spirit of God to seek God first and to keep myself physically strong. I needed to eat good food, take vitamins supplement to my diet, and exercise.

The good diet can be seen to be a strategy to fight against the enemy, so we can live a healthy and productive life.

Behold, God desires for us to be physical fit, emotional stable, and mentally aligned to his will. The earthy things will finish but the spiritual will remain. There are two destinations which are either: Hell, or Heaven.

Do the best in your daily walk with God, and do not turn back to your old and unpleasant ways.

A.   A Worthy Walk

1st Thessalonians 2:12 says, "We exhorted each one of you and encouraged you and charged you to walk in a manner worthy of God, who calls you into his own kingdom and glory".

To work worthily requires this: "Be humble, be gentle, be patient with others, live in unity with others, use your God-given gifts well, work as for the Lord, be grateful at every point in your journey, commit everything you do to God, wait patiently for the Lord, trust God to direct your steps". By Kingdom Bloggers.

According to 1 Peter 2:2, "Like new-born infants, long for the pure spiritual milk, that it you may grow up into salvation".

Godliness is living the way God wants us to live. Godly behaviour is modelled after God Himself, especially as He has revealed Himself to be the fullness of Jesus Christ.

Understanding that our conduct is the most effective way of preaching the gospel, we must conduct ourselves with prestige in the society. As it is said, a good tree is known by its fruits. A good tree will bear good fruits and a bad tree will bear bad fruits. A tree that does not produce fruits will be cut off.

We must model our lives after Jesus, imitating Him in all we do. We must understand that He is the perfect example of the love of God.

Whoever remains in Christ, will be like a tree planted by the river, he will flourish in all seasons, either bad or good. A man in Christ is a fruitful person, who will not shake or fall.

We must continually be filled with the power of the Holy Spirit, overflow with songs of praises, and thanksgiving. It's no secret that God leads us, guides, instructs, strengthens, protects, and opens our eyes and ears. He reminds us of His promises, and covenant of His glory; likewise, His honour, kingdom, and dominion.

The Lord God calls us to love one another and be good servants. We should be believers that seek to honour and reflect our godly characters in everything we do.

We should ask ourselves; "What would Jesus do?"- In any challenging situation we find ourselves in. Jesus was humble, loving-kindness, giving, faithful, and obedient.

Walking in the freedom Christ has purchased, I am learning to cherish the grace of God and not attempt to earn any by fleshly ambitions. We have received the gift to love others as an act of obedient to God.

Always do good to others when you have opportunity to do so, and sow only the things you desire to reap. God guarantees that harvest will come to you. We have to develop the heart of unity, and turn away from selfish ambitions or conceited attitudes.

Endeavor to find enjoyment in your daily work by living a quiet and peaceful life.

B. Our Responsibility

"The price of greatness is responsibility".
- Franklin D. Roosevelt

We are responsible for our conduct before men in all circumstances. We have the right to take the decision to allow God to be in our lives. Proverbs 19:20 says, "Listen to advice and accept instruction, that you may gain wisdom in the future".

Only when you let Jesus be the king of your life, that you'll have dominion to achieve the purposes of God upon your life. Confess Jesus before men and He will acknowledge you before the Father, knowing that those who have the greatest knowledge of truth will be held accountable for the fruitfulness.

We should understand we will give an account to Jesus as he is the sole Judge for every thought, word, deed, and attitude of ours. Let this influence our conduct, as God called us to live for Him.

Do we then have the responsibility to maintain love, obedience and unity? Yes, we do! John 14:15 says, "If you love Me, keep My commandments". Godliness depicts three core attributes which are Love, Obedience, and Unity.

We must recognize our body is the Temple of God; honour the devoted ministers, and make the gathering of God's people a central part of our lives. The power, the strength, the knowledge, and wisdom are given to us by the Spirit of God. Thus, we are expected to cherish this grace. The enemy will try to confuse us and bring disunity among us, but we must be vigilant and hold on to the promises of God over our lives.

We must not dwell in our former trauma, failure, and disappointment, but we shall use the gifts, and our talents to make our lives purposeful. I suffered from all, and now I have come out from the bondage I was entrapped in, to be useful for others.

Once, I lived in a place, where I had no family relatives close by to help me with any urgent issues I had. However, as God would have it, I would always receive help from my neighbour. Though, I was a stranger, my neighbours would always do their best for me to live safely. Hence, be useful to your neighbours and you will eat the fruit of their love.

They watched over me without any showing any form of discrimination towards me. My environment had rats and mouses, but these wonderful people stood beside me, and would help me sort out all my issues.

"The way of a fool is right in his own eyes, but a wise man listens to advice". - Proverbs 12:15

Personal development is our responsibility, as every job requires us to be trained to a particular level; and we are to do work in accordance to a certain expectation.

Godliness involves studying and applying the scriptures to our lives. We must stand strong in grace, and be able to say no to ungodliness; we must be self-controlled in our practice to show godly behaviour.

I examined my life and discovered my character was not tolerable, I would ask the Lord daily to deliver me from unclean spirits, pride, anger, selfishness, and judging others. I ask every day to be sanctified to enable me to walk in freedom with Christ.

Sharing Jesus with others gives us a deeper insight into the inheritance we have in Christ. Sharing your home, food, and possessions with strangers in need is a greater blessing to you who shows hospitality, than it is to the one who receives it. Practice forgiving people instantly, especially those who have offended you.

Our behaviour should make people question us that "Why do we have so much hope?" Our living involves suffering too, but we the godly people return good for evil. We learn this from Matthew 5:16 as it says, "Let your life shine so men will see your good works and glorify the Lord"

Persevere in godliness, know it is the safest virtue you can have. People who are controlled by the lusts of the flesh, have no respect for the lifestyle of the godly. Such people delight in enticing others into sin. However, God knows his elect, and will deliver them.

How do you resist temptations and be strong against worldly desires? We must endeavour to diligently avoid returning to evil practices which we have been delivered from. We must live a blameless life, be careful how we handle the word of God, and the teaching we listen to.

Remember, "Integrity is keeping a commitment even after circumstances have changed" - David Jeremiah.

C.   Endurance to the End

"No one can hit their target with their eyes closed"
- African Proverb

"Successful people maintain a positive focus in life no matter what is going on around them"
- Jack Canfield.

"I have fought the good fight, I have finished the race, I have kept the faith" - 2 Timothy 4:7

It's only after you've stepped outside your comfort zone that you begin to change, grow, and transform. I love Jesus Christ and every moment I talk to the Holy Spirit; I ask Him to help me not to sin, and now I am free. He is my best friend for life.

Now, my life has been transformed; I harbour no bitterness and resentment. I love everyone, and I have forgiven myself and others. I am learning how can I live in holiness daily; I'm learning also how to please Lord Jesus, and the Holy Spirit.

God calls us to be holy, set apart for Him, and for His purposes. Like cancer, sin can spread quickly and defile an entire church or nation.

I am learning to confront and openly confess my sin, because hiding sin will only harden our hearts. Whenever it is possible, we must make restitution for the sin we have committed against others as part of genuine repentance.

"Let us not become weary in doing good, for at the proper time we will reap the harvest if we do not give up."
- Galatians 6:9

Salvation is free for everyone, and the assurance to hear from God whenever we speak with him is also free. We use Sat-navigate or Google Maps to get to our destination when we are facing an unknown road, but we have the complete and free map to reach everywhere with the help of the Holy Spirit.

We must accept the guarantor as the Holy Spirit and trust God for everything. The way is narrow, and everyone needs self-discipline to focus on what we are called to do.

"The heart knows its own bitterness, and no stranger share its joy"
- Proverbs 14:10

"Let all bitterness and wrath and anger and clamour and slander be put away from you, along with all malice. Be kind to one another, tender-hearted, forgiving one another, as God in Christ forgave you."
- Ephesians 4:31-32

D.   Say No to Pride

"If you are filled with pride, then you will have no room for wisdom"
- African Proverb

"The reward for humility and fear of the Lord is riches and honour and life".
- Proverbs 22:4

We shall build our life upon the wisdom, the understanding and the knowledge from God Almighty.

I used to have a very defiant, and prideful attitude; I would refuse to fill up any leadership position given to me.

When I started seeking God, everything changed for me. He changed my insight and I saw my mindset slowly changing.

"Likewise, you who are younger, be subject to the elder. Clothe yourselves, all of you, with humility toward one another, for God opposes the proud but gives grace to the humble"
- 1st Peter 5:5

A humble person sees himself in the light of his relationship with Almighty God. A truly humble individual regards others more highly than himself; because his self-assessment puts others in a better perspective.

God commands us to be sober, and employ only Jesus' life and teaching, as our Godly example. We need to reassess our personal walk with God, knowing that each of us will be held accountable for our own actions.

The time I became very prosperous, I became very prideful. The reward of that attitude pushed me down and away from God. Gradually, I became miserable.

Certainly, pride will lead to a downfall. There is necessity of humility in our daily living, because God opposes a proud, and arrogant spirit. To commune with God, we must be humble, acknowledge our sins, and our need for cleansing by Him. We must understand the spirit of humility opens the pathway to fullness of joy.

In developing my humility, I was required to root out some bad manners, like retaliation.

I am healed from the trauma of 1994 genocide in Rwanda, because I humbled myself and forgave those who had sinned against me.

E.   Refrain from Evil Activities

1st Thessalonians 4:7 says, "For God has not called us for impurity, but in holiness"

We must always know true repentance involves rooting out anything that distracts us from worshipping God. I needed to eliminate any vestige of idolatry from my life.

I thoroughly disciplined myself. I understood that allowing evil activities to develop in my heart will result in an unwanted illusion, and bring unnecessary trouble into my heart.

We must further understand that God judges His people severely when they persist in the world's way of disobedience. It is advised we strive to resist any evil temptation. We must always employ the spirit when confronted with any challenge that seems beyond our control. When you involve yourself in evil activities, you are indirectly telling God he is no longer needed in your daily life.

We do not put our trust in things we have built for our security as they would be referred to as idols in our life. We should eliminate anything that serves to be represented as an idol in our daily lives.

Scriptures says in 2 Corinthians 6:16-18, "And what agreement has the temple of God with idols? For you are the temple of God of the living God. As God said: I will dwell in them, walk among them, I will be their God, and they shall be my people. Therefore, come out from them, and be separate, says the Lord. Do not touch what is unclean, and I will receive you. I will be a father to you, and you shall be My sons and My daughters says the Lord Almighty".

Our commitment is to live exclusively for God in the way He has instructed us to. To deal with chronical sins like lies, hypocrisy, sexual immorality or any unclean spirit; we have to depend on the Holy Spirit to be able to practice honesty, truth, integrity, and justice in all our interpersonal dealings.

Chapter 14
Standing as Brother's and Sister's Keeper

There is no love like the love for a brother. There is no love like the love from a brother.

"How wonderful, how beautiful when brothers and sisters get along"
- Psalms 133:1

Looking back on my own episodes in life, because I'm now redeemed and saved; I have decided to be a good sister's keeper in the kingdom of God.

My wall was fortified by good brothers, and good sisters in many ways during my journey of hardship. The Truth fights when you have a dream, and achieve your goal. With determination to do what is good, the Grace of God will lift you up.

My brother's keeper is a reference to the biblical story of Cain and Abel from the book of Genesis. It is generally understood to mean being responsible for the welfare of a brother or a sibling or by extension, for other human beings in general. Cain, who is quoted as having made this statement, claimed not to have this responsibility. However, the phrase is often used with the suggestion that people have the responsibility to care for, and watch over their fellow human beings.

Cain and Abel were sons of Adam and Eve. Cain, a farmer, and Abel, a shepherd; Each sacrificed the fruits of their labour to God. God looked favourably upon Abel's sacrifice, but not Cain's, and in his anger over that, Cain killed his brother. Someone who is his brother's keeper looks out for and cares for others, even if they are not actually related to him or her.

For example, a person who tries to be a brother's keeper might donate his or her time, or resources to help others and will place the needs of others before his or her own.

We all have brothers and sisters; biological, spiritual, or just friendly people who we consider as brothers or sisters. Some will make an impact in your life, while some won't.

Love all your family members and be a blessing, not a curse to them. After, my university studies, I worked and saved my earnings to give a pleasant gift to my father. The gift was to buy a house for Him before my marriage.

My mum died earlier and left us as young children. The youngest child was two years, and six months when she died. The only thing she could recognize then was a t-shirt belonging to my mom.

Every time she looked at this t-shirt, she cried. I knew I had to hide the shirt until it got destroyed in the 1994 genocide. My father refused to marry again, for He vowed to protect us from harm. My late father looked after all of us till we reached a matured age.

This was his statement then" I will not allow any other woman to disgrace or mistreat my children. It is better to remain single and take care of the fruits of my womb".

The devil is a killer, destroyer and robber. Be aware of him and do not commit your offspring to God. My sister gave birth when she was the ripe age of a teenager. As our sister's keeper, my siblings and I took up the responsibility to take care of her. We dedicated ourselves to look after our sister till she finished her studies.

When somebody has a great destiny, then enemy will set a snare for the person to stop going forward. No doubt, my sister had a great destiny, and today she has been a blessing to many generations and nations. Be a faithful servant of God without complaining or arguing. Make sacrifices to assist your siblings, and in due time they will be your stepping step and rescue you from despair.

During the post genocide in Rwanda, she came to comfort me from a foreign country by bringing new clothes to cover my nakedness. Observing the hard situations that I was living in;

she offered all the support she could to my broken family.

When I newly arrived in Europe, I didn't have any money to buy bread, and when I spoke to her, she sent me some money instantly for me to survive with.

Having a good sister is the best thing. Be not isolated from your sisters or brothers because they are the source of your blessings.

We should avoid being selfish, and look unto the best interest for saving the life of someone. Often, I had terrific people who I referred to as my keepers; they helped me survive at different times.

There was a time, I was supposed to go for an internship, but I didn't have clothes to wear. My sister married and my auntie clothed me with her best clothes. I was able to succeed in my duty, with confidence.

Can you be a sacrificial person for your siblings?

When my mom died and my dad got widowed, my teenage sister abandoned her studies to allow me continue in university. She made sacrifices by interrupting her academics, and she stayed at home to look after our family. She played the role of a mother and looked after my young brothers, sisters, and our dad.

Our teenager brother became very sick and almost died. My sister saw this and quickly carried him on her back to the nearest clinic.

It is very good to make a difference and rescue a soul. All the souls she fought for, have become men and women of great destinies, and have borne fruits to all generation.

I would encourage everyone to have excellent relationship with good friends.

My female best friend gave her life to save, and shield my children by moving them to a foreigner's country for their safety. She abandoned her belongings, houses, and family for my support.

We are here on earth to do good work and to care for one another. We should not neglect our sisters and brothers, but rather find a way to make peace and attend to their needs; either emotionally, spiritually, or physically.

Choose to be your brother's keeper in your community; in your nuclear family and extended family. Be sensitive to their wellbeing. Let us be ready to give, forgive, and receive others back without grumbling or murmuring.
No matter how big or small your future is; it belongs to God, and in due time you will eat the fruit of your labour.

Everyone around us; either our spiritual sister, spiritual brother or best friend – all deserve respect, honour, love, and dignity.

After experiencing the death of my loved ones, I came across one of my friends who helped me rush to a safe place. They helped me search for food and water, and even strengthened me as a low state survivor.

Do your miracles always seem like a dream? Sometimes, I live a miraculous life that seems like a dream, but I know it's the Lord's hand at work in my life.

One of my siblings decided to come to the field and have eye contact with the realities of the casualties. After my Rwandan battle in 1994, my brother, Kayijuka; moved with compassion came from Bujumbura /Burundi to Mugina/ Rwanda.

He travelled on road and walked many miles, searching everywhere for me from one camp to another. He described how I looked like to dozens of people. I had a scar on my neck then, and my brother knew. He was using the scar as a distinguishing mark to describe me to people.

Later, he confirmed from people that I was still alive. He came to have reassurance, if I was still alive or dead, for he had received telling him I was as good as dead.

On the day I finally saw my brother, I remember I was standing outside and mashing herbs to eat. I saw a shadow of a man but I didn't pay attention to him, because I was very busy. Suddenly, I lifted my eyes and I recognised it was my biological brother.

This circumstance taught and revealed to me that I was not alone, though I was lost, yet God brought my brother to comfort me.

It was a miracle to see him and I couldn't believe he was with me. I had never dreamt to be visited by my own relatives in that rescuing place. He was afraid to approach me, as he was told that I was mentally sick. He walked closer to me gently, to be absolutely sure I wasn't.

It was a glorious encounter and from that moment, I knew in my heart the genocide had finished.

Display the Unconditional Love

Can we die for someone? Can we make sacrifices for others?

We must know that one who has unreliable friends soon comes to ruin, but there is a friend who sticks closer than a brother.

The genociders haunted me everywhere to have me killed. They went to investigate and asked the late priest of the Juvenal of Catholic Church at Muhanga, for my whereabouts.

For my protection, he refused to disclose where I was hiding, and the killers killed him because of that. Proverbs 17: 17 says "A friend loves at all the times, and a brother is born for a time of adversity".

This young man had a noble character of a brother's keeper, and sacrificed his life for me. He was a true Christian that feared God, and a good brother's keeper.

I have been given the duty to tell everyone to always have mercy on others, and be a divine helper to others during hopeless times. We should endeavour to stay connected to good people with love, joy, peace and faith.

True Christians suffer for others, and accept to die on behalf of others. Our late best friend, Rubuye, was slaughtered as he refused to hand over his late wife, Ingabire.

I came across a Rwandan compatriot, who eventually became my best friend. Her name is Pastor Pauline Kanzayire. She encouraged me in all areas of my life by praying with me and for me without ceasing.

In good times and bad times, always be prepared to fight spiritual battles.

I remember in the beginning of the pandemic in 2019, I became sick, and when she heard that I was unwell, she ran to my house and met an ambulance team coming to rescue me.

She wasn't scared of getting contaminated by COVID-19. She put on the full armour of God, and all the personal protective equipment to support me during this phase. The worries filled all my children, even though I was not later diagnosed from COVID-19.

The Bible says in Revelation 12:11, "To put on the armour of God is to apply all the gospel to all your life." The whole armour of God is the expression of full trust in God and what He has done for you through Jesus Christ. Your victory in spiritual warfare was secured at the cross of Jesus and the blood that was shed.

Find faithful, godly, and fearful friends, and you will grow strong; for iron sharpens iron.

"As iron sharpens iron, so a man sharpens the countenance of his friend" - Proverbs 27:17

My prayer is for the Lord to transform our heart for His glory. Do not hate your sister or your brother, instead make peace and fight the good fight with them.

There is an abundance of blessings to connect with good sisters and good brothers.

We are called by God to be good ambassadors.

I aim to speak to nations, and generations about the importance of having a good brother as a keeper. A brother's keeper that is filled with compassion, kindness, patience, faithfulness, humility, joy, and love.

I have been rescued and saved to tell people to love one another, and to be a good brother's keeper. God will look favourably upon you, if you care for others.

Chapter 15
Resultant the Peace

"No matter how long the night, the day is sure to come"
- Congolese Proverb

The Hand of God is always upon me and all around me; to give me peace which surpasses all understanding to build my family

Exodus 15:6 says, "Your right hand, oh Lord, glorious in power, your right hand oh Lord, shatters the enemy.

1st Peter 5:6-7 says, "Humble yourselves, therefore, under the mighty hand of God so that at the proper time he may exalt you. Cast all your anxieties on Him, for He cares for you."

A.   Exhumation and Memorial

"In remembering the Holocaust, we should think about what we can do as individuals to prevent genocide. That is the best way to honour the victims"
- Dr Jean Damascene Bizimana.

The Truth will continue to fight for all of us and overcome circumstances such as; lack of peace, rejection, trauma, heartbreak, self-isolation, unforgiveness, and hatred. My continuous journey with faith, holiness, humility, dedication to live and bear good fruits, has given me a new state of life.

I now stand bravely as the only surviving adult in my entire family (in-law) to fight the good fight on their behalf.

In the year 2022, I was revived to do my duty of burying my late husband and son in an appropriate and honourable place. They were both killed in the 1994 genocide against the Tutsi. The preparation required a lot of emotional, physical and spiritual support, because I had to breakdown their previous graves located on the main road to take their bodies to the right place.

How could I have achieved this horrible task after twenty-eight years of their death? Indeed, with God all things are possible.

I spent forty days fasting and asking God for strength, and courage to overcome my fear of acceptance. Back in August 1994, I didn't want to see the dead body of my late husband because of this same fear.

During the period of fasting and prayer, I did not consult with anyone as I wanted God to tell me what to do. I solely kept to myself; seeking the face of the Lord on how to effectively deal with the situation at hand. On completion, I felt a great peace in my heart. I decided with confidence to do the appropriate and honourable funeral of my late husband and son through the grace of God.

The success of the entire process was owed to faithful relatives, friends, families, the government represented by the mayor of the district, all members of the survivor's association of IBUKA, all ex-students of ACEJ, Karama, Muhanga District, all surviving friends of late Nyagatare Joseph, and the Congregation of New Life International Church Manchester, United Kingdom.

IBUKA, which means, "Remember," is a non-government association, founded on 14th December, 1995. Its main mission is to preserve the memory of the genocide against Tutsi and to defend rights and interests of survivors across the country.

IBUKA is an umbrella, or an organization for the surviving genocide individuals in Rwanda. IBUKA is independent, non-profit oriented, and is legally recognized by the government of Rwanda. By remembering the past, we can help the survivors, and we can help also the generations to come to live in peace."

I am grateful and thankful to have the IBUKA represented by Naptali Ahishakiye; The National Executive, Muhanga Kayitesi Beata; Vice President of Ibuka of District, Mugaga Jonhson, Ufitikirezi Alphonsine and by Mayer Jacky Kayitesi.

On July 21, 2022, our grieving over our beloved started, but with the steadfast spirit of God, the devil was defeated. The exercise to dig out the ground and search for the dead bodies started, and took nearly five hours. The population came around and some helped me to intercede with prayers, and worship God with songs.

Exhumation of the bodies

Top Left: Late Joseph Nyagatare and David Ricardo, buried on the main road
Top Right: Removal from the grave
Bottom Left: Placement of the bodies by best friends and the relative survivors
Bottom Right: Taking the bodies to the appropriate place to be honoured

My consciousness of the process increased with reassurance that all my relatives, and off springs were standing without any drop of tears. I was to firstly identify the bones in the ground, which confirmed their entire bodies were alright after five hours of searching.

We identified only the main skeleton, and the bones were almost decayed; equally their clothes. I saw with my eyes the confirmation of the word of God that says, "We are dust and to dust we shall return".

I appreciated the love and kindness from the members of the IBUKA organisation, and also from the Rwandan population who stood by to monitor all the process.

Surely, you shall see the goodness of the Lord in the land of the living when you least expect it. There was a moment, when one of the members from the Rwandan population had to hold me, so I wouldn't collapse.

This kind of love demonstrated to me that I was surrounded with people who oved and cared for me deeply.

Faithfulness is the key to honour our vows. After seeing and hearing all the evil propaganda against him as a noble Tutsi school headmaster through the mass media, my husband knew he was going to die and had nowhere to hide.

I vividly remember him telling me to wash him clean after his death.

On the 21st day in July, 2022- I decided to honour my vows and wash the decayed bodies. I participated and was assisted by members of IBUKA to wash the bodies. I thank God I was able to identify the bullet left from the shooting on his crane.

Bullet found in the crane of my late husband

Members Of IBUKA and myself washing clothes

The Rest of their Clothes Washed

There will always be a way out when it seems there is no way.

After washing the skeleton and bones, I was persuaded to leave them to dry at the memorial room for three days before transferring it to be in the coffin. Miraculously, a precious woman called Patrice Barakagwira and her husband François Kayijuka, stood up and gave me a bedroom within their house to allow the bodies to dry.

Then, I was able to wait and watch the skeletons dry until we placed them in the coffin.

B.   Back to Memories

We were overwhelmed with the healing and the restoration of peace for all of us.

Everyone was genuinely thrilled to be back in Rwanda, and used the opportunity to explore the goodness of God over the country. Even though, it was previously destroyed in 1994, it is now one of the best places for safety and peace.

On July 24, 2022, my children wished to see one of the places where God rescued me, and their late Father's workplace.

I had never journeyed back to visit the places after twenty-eight years, for I had no peace. Once again, I was anointed with power and peace to narrate my ordeals to my family about the place.

We visited the altar with gratitude, and joy. We walked within the Cathedral Kabgayi, St Joseph College, and Petit Seminaire Saint Leon-Kabgayi Seminary in Kabgayi. My children were more than excited.

One of my children, Peter Nyagatare, who was once rescued from the place had a nightmare there, but the visit became a stepping hill to heal him from his trauma.

We had the privilege to meet a tour guide, who took us around and showed us the premises. We were able to visit the place were women taken from St. Joseph were raped before they were killed. My children testified the place stunk from the odour of dead bodies.

The journey was exciting, but was also an emotional moment

for me. It reminded me to never forget the goodness of God, who put an end to the 1994 Genocide in Rwanda

We reached our final destination which was the ACEJ High School College. The children walked around the premises and saw the office of their late father. They saw the monument built in memory of the killed students, teachers and of their father, Joseph Nyagatare.

A Memorial placed in ACEJ School; For the students, teachers and late headmaster, my ex-husband, Joseph Nyagatare killed in the 1994 Genocide.

The génocidaires killed 46 students, 4 teachers and a headmaster. I am learning to forget the former things and see God's goodness, faith, and hope

I appreciated this act of remembrance. We were able to visit many places and it was joyful seeing houses in Rwanda were all built with modern materials.

C.   Unforgettable Day

On June 25, 2022, my dream came true when I buried my late husband, and my son, David Ricardo Nyagatare, at the Memorial Site in Kicukiro, Nyanza Kigali, Rwanda, after twenty-eight years.

We had such a great time of grieving, and then celebrating their lives with friends, families, survivors, and neighbours from the country and from abroad.

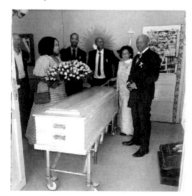

Late Nyagatare at the memorial site in Kicukiro, Nyanza, Kigali

D. Leaving The Legacy

A lot of people, friends, and relatives came to give their testimonies about my late husband, Joseph Nyagatare. Many souls came from far and near, because of the excellent memories he left behind.

I appreciated all ex-students who were present on the day to testify about his works as a noble headteacher. These ex-students have set apart a day, every year to celebrate to remember the good works and the gentleness of their late headmaster, ex-students, and ex-teachers of the college who were killed during the genocide.

Some testimonies from students, who survived the 1994 genocide:

1st Alumni: The student testified of how she was falsely accused for having knifes, and poisoning meals; in order to kill other students in Hutu. Her late headmaster, Joseph Nyagatare, comforted her not to be shaken because it was a fake propaganda against her.

2nd Alumni: She testified how the students protested against the committee members of the school to protect Joseph, after he was being greatly persecuted. The students stood up and supported their headmaster, as he was a great man leading the school.

3rd Alumni: The student testified the late Joseph punished students by asking the one with fault, to find something good to do; to erase the wrong doing. This method of correction originated from a saying which is "Bad actions are erased by good actions" In French - "Les mauvaises actions s'effacent par les bonnes actions".

4th Alumni (currently the Mayor of District): He testified, "I finished primary school but I got obstructed to continue as I was a Tutsi. My father took me to the late headmaster of ACEJ, and he gave me a place in the academy to further my education.

We heard many testimonies from amazing friends such as; Nsabimpuhwe Venuste, Gahongayire Yusufu, Masumbuko François, and Rustibuka Innocent, who all said how good and noble he was.

The funeral day was so great because everyone spoke of the legacy he left behind. Though the children grieved a lot for their late father and late brother, for it was their first moment of hearing all the harsh realities involved in their father's and brother's death. Still, they were very pleased to hear of their father's exploits.

We were finally at peace, and we truly celebrated that with family, friends, all compatriots, many alumni of the class of 1994, teachers, colleagues from different communities, and IBUKA members.

I'm more than thankful for the effort made by the government to establish memorial site all over the country to honour our beloved; who were killed either for being Tutsi or Hutu.

We are no longer divided in Rwanda; we are unified under one umbrella.

In one accord, the celebration was done in harmony. We finished the event all standing in one union singing: "Magnificat Roho Yanjye Irasingiza Nyagasani" (Meaning My Soul is Praising the Lord God).

The hand of God was upon each one of us, and his presence was in our midst.

Conclusion
Word Declaration & Power of Faith

The word of our mouth is the only key that can destroy or save us; it can also be the key to our victory or to our failures. The declaration of God's word was always my armour during hardships such as during the 1994 genocide, childbirth deliverance, and so many more.

Confronting any situation requires us to acknowledge God, to direct, guide, give us wisdom and a discerning spirit. Stay alert to the Holy Spirit who guides, instructs, leads, and strengthens in all ways.

God will never leave, nor forsake His people.

We are here on earth to take dominion, to multiply and live daily by fellowshipping with the Lord. We are all on a journey, and we are heading to either Heaven, or to Hell. Choose the right way and if you are doubting, ask God frequently to manifest and reveal the truth to you. He is listening to our heart desires and His will must be fulfilled.

Ask divine helpers, who are spiritually matured in God to pray and help you spiritually. Never despise the elders, leaders, pastors, prophets, apostles, teachers, and evangelists, because they have been chosen by God to guide us.

Everyone is an ambassador of God, and the Lord Jesus Christ. Sometimes, many unbelievers or lukewarm Christians live under curses because of lack of knowledge.

I am learning every day to accept corrections and be kind to others who are weak.

Galatians 6:1 says "Brothers, if anyone is caught in any transgressions, you who are spiritual should restore him in a spirit of gentleness. Keep watch on yourself, lest you too be tempted".

There was a time, I disagreed to what a pastor was saying, because God had told me something different entirely. While I was doubting and arguing, God spoke to me directly and I suddenly opened my Bible to find the confirmation of what I was saying.

Our tongue is the giver of life, or death. Your tongue can save you, if you choose the right words of blessings, and not curses.

Nobody can ever change me, only God can. I believe in Jesus Christ, and I quickly repent whenever I commit a sin.

Whenever I speak the word of God in any situation, I see the moving Hand of God in the situation. Praise God, who rescues us and saves us to be used as his vessels in proclaiming the gospel of good news to unbelievers.

The journey of life will continue, but we know we will be okay because we have God on our side. We must practice daily what the word says.

Today, I am grateful and thankful to God for moving me from glory to glory. I can boldly affirm that I am forgiven, and I have forgiven everyone who has offended me. In life, there will be tribulations, but we shall overcome them all because Christ has won the battle for us.

I pray for all my Rwandan compatriots to live healthy lives; full of forgiveness and God's goodness. In Rwanda, there is no more discrimination in diversity, religion, and amongst ethnic groups.

Any form of harassment, discrimination, and segregation is from Satan. The way back to Him is only through thorough repentance from God.

I have forgiven all those who participated in the killing of my beloved late husband, my friends, and my entire in-laws. I found out it was a satanic plan from the devil to extinguish the Tutsi population, but the Truth fought the devil and won. Today, Rwandan people are unified as one nation.

I am a living vessel to proclaim the good news of Salvation; declaring and decreeing God's words over any situation before me. The Truth that fought the genocide in Rwanda, has trained me to testify to the goodness of God.

Fight for the truth, and examine your heart to know if you are being genuine to the will of God.

The Truth will always bring you into unexpected victory. The forces Army RPF (Front Patriotic Rwandan), won the battle because they were fighting for the human rights of Tutsi People. I was not ready yet to die, and the Truth fought for me. Now, I am a living testimony.

Reject all evil devices of separation, limitation, manipulation, and bad political interests promoting discrimination and diversities.

I will never forget one of the statements I said during the genocide, "Oh God, for the extreme suffering of our Lord Jesus, have mercy upon us and upon the whole world" These words have the power to fight any battle.

The Truth will always fight for you; you only need to stand in faith, and speak God's word. I remember the story of Daniel in the den of lions, the faith of Moses in the wilderness, and David who was always after God's heart.

Walk in the supernatural by eating the word of God daily; and you shall not be shaken for you walk by faith, not by sight.

Here are some powerful scriptures that are weapons to hold unto during trials, and challenges:

- 1 Corinthians 1:9; "God is faithful, by whom you were called into the fellowship of His Son, Jesus Christ, our Lord".

- Numbers 23:19, "God is not a man, that He should lie, nor a son of man, that He should repent. He has said, and will not do? Or has He spoken, and will He not make it good".

- Genesis 28:15, "Behold, I am with you and will keep you wherever you go, and will bring you back to this land; for I will not leave until I have done what I have spoken to you".

- Deuteronomy 7:9, "Therefore know that the Lord your God, He is God, the faithful God who keeps covenant and mercy for thousand generations with those who loves Him and keep His commandments".

- John 14:6, "Jesus said, I am the way, the truth, and the life. No one comes to the father except through Me".

- 2 Timothy 2:11-13, "This is the faithful saying: For if we die with Him, we shall also live with Him. If we endure with Him, we shall also reign with Him. If we deny Him, He also will deny us. If we are faithful, He remains faithful; He cannot deny Himself".

- Hebrews 13:8, "Jesus is the same yesterday, today, and forever".

- Isaiah 40:8, "The grass withers, the flower fades, but the word of our God stands forever".

- Philippians 4:6, "Be anxious for nothing, but in everything by prayer and supplication, with thanksgiving, let your request be made known to God".

- Romans 8:31, "What then shall we say to these things? If God is for us, who can be against us?"

- Proverbs 3:5-7, "Trust in the Lord with all your heart; and lean not to your own understanding. In all our ways acknowledge Him, and He shall direct our steps. Do not be wise in your own eyes; fear the Lord and depart from evil".

Speak with confidence and trust the Lord; Know who you are and work out your salvation. Also, examine your life and call upon the father, who will never leave you nor forsake you.

For the Lord is my light and my salvation; whom shall I be afraid of?

"One thing I desired from the Lord, was that I would dwell in the house of the Lord – All the days of my life, to behold the beauty of the Lord and to inquire in his temple." - Psalm 27:4

People are living under the addiction of drugs and alcohol. They have temporal peace and have missed their destiny, for they do not have the Spirit of God to guide, protect and to lead them right.

Forgiveness and repentance are the keys to opening the doors of wellbeing in our lives.

I lived a life of forgiveness, and whenever I offended someone, my next action would be to kneel and repent of my sins. Then, I would go back to the person offended, and beg for their forgiveness.

"Finally brethren, whatever things are true, noble, just, whatever things are pure, lovely, of good report, if there is anything praise worthy meditate on these things".
- Philippians 4:8

Affirmations you should say daily

I am a child of God in Christ; I will live and not die before my time. I am more than a conqueror in Christ; I am blessed and highly favoured.

I am strong and powerful in Christ; I am fearful and wonderful made.

I am anointed and equipped; empowered by God to do good works.

I am prosperous and successful.

I am the redeemed of the lord; I am free from condemnation.

I am forgiven, reconciled, and I forgive others who hurt me.

I am thankful you blessed me with spiritual blessings.

I am loved.

I am healed and restored to God's glory.

I am walking with the Lord.

I am a vessel for God in His kingdom.

I am a new creation in Christ.

I am faithful and thankful to God.

I am for signs and wonders; the light and salt of the earth.

I am grateful to God for my life, and for what He has done.

No weapon forged against me shall prosper.

Believing in Christ, the Saviour, is the only way to have access to our spiritual blessings; for we would have the Guarantor if we do so, and the Holy Spirit will enable us to have access to all our needs in life.

Sins can serve as a blockage to our destinies. We are to invite God to take possession of our life and let Him rule over our life. The spirit of God will cast out from our lives all bad habits; like telling lies, stealing, envying, jealousness, pornography, pride, anger, bitterness, addiction to alcohol, addiction to seduction, sexual immorality, masturbation, fornication, gossiping, backbiting, smoking of cigarette and any other intoxicating drugs, manipulation, and idolatry.

If you can deliver yourself from any of these, you will see the Hand of God in your life, and live happily. Anything you do in secret will be exposed. Let us be committed to God and focus on fearing, loving, obeying, and seeking Him.

These are the weapons used by the devil to pull people away from God. God has set me free from the snare of all of them. He rescued and saved me to tell nations, and generations about him.

The key is to repent, confess the name of Jesus, believe he died for you, and he will give you a new life.

The Truth that fights stopped the 1994 genocide against Tutsi in Rwanda. During the mass killing, I stood in faith without ceasing in prayer. The intensive prayer I prayed during that period, is what gave me the victory I have today. Let the Truth that fights your battle sharpen your tongue.

Make these declarations with faith and expect multiple blessings

I have the grace I need for today. I will not worry; I will not doubt. I will keep my trust in God, knowing that he will not fail me.

I will be an opportunity to encourage others.

I will speak the word of faith; I am full of power and strength.

I will overcome every obstacle, and every challenge.

He is directing my steps; all situations work out every detail for my advantage.

I will look for what is right, and not what is wrong.

I will sing each day as my heart will overflow with his praises, and gratitude for all His goodness.

I will lift the fallen, restore the broken, and encourage the discouraged.

Our obligations

- We must be confident that God honours those who depend upon His wisdom, and carry out the work He assigned for them to do.

- We must be confident, that if we seek God with all our heart, our soul and spirit, He will surely be found. Faithfully apply God's Word to your life.

- We must maintain a heart that is fully committed to the Lord; seek God's face continually, and prayerfully for every decision we make.

- We must be assured the Lord's promises are for those whose hearts are fully committed to Him. Psalms 32:8, "I will instruct you and teach you the way you should go; I will counsel you with my eye upon you".

- We must be careful, not to let those things whom we have affection for, lead us away from full devotion to the Lord.

The grace of God and His mercy are near those that have a willing heart to live godly lives. We shall say we are the head and not the tail; winners and not failures.

To all readers, spread this message across to other readers:

Anyone who has gone astray from his family, and is frightened to go back to his family in his motherland due to one reason or another, should look back and listen to God's word to get peace.

For twenty-eight years, I was isolated, entangled, enslaved, and bounded with satanic chains, because of the hallucinations and trauma I had that were linked to the 1994 genocide against the Tutsi in Rwanda. I could not imagine myself socializing again with anyone in Rwanda.

The complete healing through the power of God has enabled me to love, and go back to socialise with my fellow compatriots in Rwanda.

God is transforming difficult lives into pleasant testimonies, for the Truth will always fight for you. I have been forgiven by God, and reconciled to him. I have also forgiven all the genocide murderers.

I am a living testimony, and a survivor of the 1994 genocide against the Tutsi population in Rwanda. I'm now completely healed from despair. I live a new life, and my confidence is built on the fact that there is no condemnation for those who are in Christ.

Know the Truth, find the Truth, live in the Truth; for the Truth always wins the battle.

About the Author

I heard several times that there is light out of a tunnel. But for 100 days, from April to July 1994, there was no light in Rwanda. The country plunged into darkness. A planned, deliberate and systematic mass-killing targeted the Tutsi population and more than 1million of them were brutally slaughtered mainly by machetes by fellow citizens in a state-led genocide. I survived that human madness and this book is the crossing of my valley of death.

We were fearfully waiting in the antechamber of death like sheep queuing for the slaughter. From hopelessness and despair a glimmer of hope kept me alive. The desire to live was burning in me. Clinging on an eventual divine rescue helped me to survive the ordeal. In the name of my offspring I wanted to survive and bring them up. I prayed "The Lord's Prayer" thousand times. I invented some survival tactics which bought me some time: I behaved as a fool in the midst of other survivors.

I believe that I was rescued and left to tell the story of those lives that were stolen, mutilated, raped before their final breath. 1994 Genocide against Tutsi was a culmination of a long list of atrocities Tutsi people suffered since 1959. Second-class citizens, longstanding socio-economic and political discrimination and exclusion and then a state-led Genocide. I still have my "whys" still not answered after 29 years. I have wounds even now in the process of healing. But I am glad God is in charge and He has already changed me into a new person able to forgive and move on. I have resettled in UK and I am happy mum to all my children and grandchildren.

The purpose and intention of sharing this book is to ensure that the future generations are well informed and never forget the extreme atrocities that more than one million innocent people experienced in the 1994 genocide against Tutsi in Rwanda. This is a small story but it is a story of many who could not tell their stories. In their name I decided to tell my story, so that one day the "Never Again" will have a meaning.

Deborah Munganyinka Simugomwa

Truth that Fights

A survivor's Memoir of the 1994 Genocide against Tutsi in Kabgayi, Rwanda

Autobiography by Deborah Munganyinka Simugomwa

Divine helpers that assisted me in writing this book:
Pastor David O. Nnadede, Mr Ralph Segum, and Cinthia Iradukunda

References:

The Holy Bible, New International Version (niv) 2011 by Biblica, formerly International Bible Society.

God's promises for your every need (New King James Version 1982 by Thomas Nelson), scripture quotations taken 2006, 2019.

The Holy Bible, King James Version (2014), Bible Society of Nigeria

Wiersbe, W.W, Prayer, Praise & Promises; A Daily Walk through the Psalms. Copyright 1992.

Initial editors of this book:
Pastor David Nadede & Mr Raphael

Design, Editing, Proof-reading and Print:
Schribe Publishing Ltd, London
www.schribepublishing.com